Bill & Bev Beatty's

WILD PLANT COOKBOOK

Illustrations by Bev Beatty.

by Bill Beatty

Library of Congress Cataloging in Publication Data
Beatty, Bill, 1948—
    Bill & Bev Beatty's wild plant cookbook.

    Bibliography: p.
    Includes index.
    1. Cookery (Wild foods) 2. Wild plants, Edible. I. Title.
II. Title: Bill and Bev Beatty's wild plant cookbook. III. Wild
plant cookbook.
TX823.B423   1987   641.6   87-7802

ISBN 0-87961-158-8
ISBN 0-87961-159-6 (pbk.)

Books for a better world

Naturegraph Publishers, Inc.
P.O. Box 1075
Happy Camp, CA 96039
U.S.A.

To my father,
who took me fishing;
and my grandmother,
who tolerated worms in my pockets.

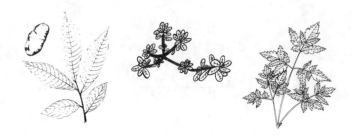

Table of Contents

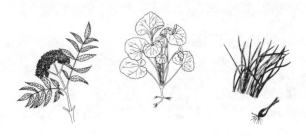

Acknowledgements

My outlook on life and the way I view the natural world has, more than anything else, influenced the writing of this book. II Corinthians 5:17 describes it best:

Therefore, if any one is in Christ, he is a new creation; the old has passed away, behold, the new has come.

I am compelled to acknowledge nature itself. The following best describes my feelings and experiences concerning the natural world:

You shall know the night—its space, its light, its music. You shall see earth sink in the darkness and the universe appear. No roof shall shut you from the presence of the moon. You shall see mountains rise in the transparent shadow before dawn. You shall see—and feel—You shall enter the living shelter of the forest. You shall walk where only the wind has walked before. You shall know immensity, and see continuing the primeval forces of the world. You shall know not one small segment, but the whole of life—strange, miraculous, living, dying, changing. You shall see storms arise, and drenched and deafened, shall exalt in them. You shall top a rise and behold creation. And you shall need the tongues of angels to tell what you have seen.

Author Unknown

Only one other person was directly involved in this endeavor, my wife, Bev. She proofed, edited, suggested, tasted, tested, and right in the middle of it all, had our third child. She withstood my late nights of typing, the times I turned myself off to all around me, and my countless trips to the woods. This book is every bit as much hers as mine.

Two people enkindled my interest in botany and edible wild plants. The late M.H. Berry, my college plant taxonomy instructor, instilled in me an insatiable desire to identify everything, and Wilma Bruhn inspired me with her level of activity and her knowledge of edible wild plants.

I am also grateful for the works by the late Euell Gibbons. His books, *Stalking The Wild Asparagus* and *Stalking The Healthful Herbs,* have been my frequent companions. Similarly I am indebted to Dr. Earl Core and P.D. Strausbaugh (both now deceased) for *Flora of West Virginia.*

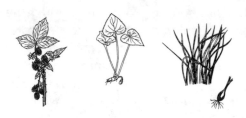

Preface

I have been teaching about edible wild plants for more than ten years. During this time some of my workshop participants have become discouraged when they take off to the woods to forage on their own. They feel inadequate when it comes to identifying and collecting wild foods. Some of the wild food guides available today are very good, but they can be overwhelming. For many folks, it is too much too soon. Many of the plants listed are not that common throughout the United States, at least not in large enough quantities to rely upon as an occasional food source. Some plants listed in the field guides do not taste good. This can be a big letdown after having invested hard-earned money and sometimes a great deal of time learning about edible wild plants.

I included the wild plants contained in this guide because they stand on their own merit. These are the best of the wild food plants because of their tastes, nutritional values, and availability. Also, most are easy to identify.

I eat wild foods because they are free, nutritious, good tasting and most of all, they are fun. My family and I enjoy being outdoors together. Collecting edible wild plants gets us outdoors more often. Edible wild plants are not a main-stay in my diet. I'm more interested in the identification and natural history of plants than in the taste. Bev and I create good tasting edible wild plant recipes as a form of entertainment rather than for survival. At some future date I may eat nothing but wild plants for a month, six months, or even a year; but because of present family and professional responsibilities, this adventure is still a dream.

This field guide is not intended to teach plant indentification. Good books on the topic of plant identification do not deal with the edibilitiy of plants; they deal only with the identification process. I spent 96 hours in a plant taxonomy class, not learning the identification of all the plants in my area but instead learning the *process* of plant identification. Once you learn *how,* you can begin cataloging all those plant names in your mind, and you won't need to spend the time that I did. I just happen to have a fatal case of what you might call "What's that over there?" I thoroughly enjoy learning the names of mushrooms, birds, flowering plants—really, anything alive. Would-be wild food enthusiasts should get a copy of Peterson's *Field Guide to Wildflowers* or *Newcomb's Wildflower Guide.* Either of these guides should be adequate for plant identification purposes.

My interest in the outdoors has been part of me ever since I can remember. My excitement in wild plants as a food source began in a plant taxonomy class at college. When I first heard the English equivalent of the dandelion's botanical name, I became overwhelmed with the desire to learn more about the edible and medicinal qualities of the wild plants in eastern North America. Just before graduating from college, I committed myself to a full-time naturalist's position. One of the most popular classes taught at the nature center where I began my career was "Edible Wild Foods." Since then I have acquired many, many personal experiences with edible wild plants, *all* of them enjoyable.

This book was written for the casual as well as for the serious wild food forager. One can have fun with the plants found in the following pages. Or, for the survival-minded, a diet of nothing but edible wild foods over a long period of time is possible because of the wide geographical range of the plants in this text.

The recipes are a result of much thought, time, experimentation, and fun. Some are domestic vegetable recipes adapted to wild plants. Others are new creations which complement the taste and character of the individual plants. Be creative with recipes. Try new methods of cooking, use spices and herbs, and substitute wherever possible. Some successful substitutions are: Ramps in place of onions; poke, lamb's quarters, and nettles for spinach; Jerusalem artichokes instead of potatoes; chickweed and violet leaves for lettuce; milkweed broccoli in place of broccoli; Cossack asparagus for cucumber or if cooked, in place of asparagus. We were pleasantly surprised at the outcome of most of our experiments.

More and more people are working toward some form of self-sufficiency. They want to be prepared for any major economic difficulties that the future may hold. To me, being prepared has to do with independence and conservation. Gardening skills such as composting and planting seed saved from the previous year, canning and drying food—in other words, becoming less dependent upon our present food system—are all part of becoming self-sufficient. A knowledge of edible wild plants has added a great deal to my independence, especially when those wild food plants are abundant where I live, taste good, and have most of the vitamins and minerals my body needs to exist. Robert Rodale wrote, "Soil is better than gold!" (*Organic Gardening Magazine*, January, 1980.) I believe that a knowledge of edible wild plants and other survival-related skills can be applied to what Mr. Rodale is saying about good garden soil.

My knowledge of wild food plants is very valuable toward attaining my goal: Independence from our present food system. My family grows most of our own food. We do not depend upon wild food plants as our food source; but if the occasion ever arises, our knowledge of wild food plants will aid in supplying our food and necessary nutrients.

All plants were at one time wild. Fruits and vegetables found in the supermarkets are nothing more than domesticated wild food plants. Some of the plants included in the following pages are occasionally found in the produce section of many supermarkets. Since the American public is becoming increasingly concerned with health and nutrition, I wouldn't be surprised to see some of these wild "nutritional treasure houses" become regular additions to many individual's diets. Until this time arrives, I shall continue to forage and reap the benefit of the sounds of singing birds, dew-laden spider webs, the beauty of countless trilliums in springtime—the glory of all creation. In a way, I hope wild food plants always remain wild.

Edible Wild Plant Nutrition

Health is life. There is nothing as important to our physical well-being as nutrition. Physical ailments can often be caused by a lack of the proper amount of a certain vitamin or mineral, but these ailments are sometimes diagnosed as being caused by other factors. Instead of keying in on the recurring problem, some physicians will treat only the symptom, even though the cure may be obtained by a simple dietary change. Therefore, it is very important to keep our bodies healthy by eating the right foods. Many health problems in the United States today are considered to be caused by eating too much of the wrong foods or too little of the right foods.

Edible wild plants can provide much of our body's most necessary nutrition. Edible wild plants are *free* sources of vitamins and minerals. They are, more often than not, higher sources than similar domestic vegetables. The plants listed in this field guide are available to millions of people. There is no work or time involved in planting, transplanting, watering, mulching, weeding, or insect control—only harvesting. I can think of no easier way to combat inflation and supplement one's daily nutritional intake.

The nutritional analysis of violet leaves, Shepherd's purse, bird rape, stinging nettle, mint *(Mentha sp.)*, and day lily were compiled from "How Good Are Wild Foods?" by Robert Shosteck, in *The Mother Earth News*, Issue No. 60, 1979. The analysis of all other plants was compiled from *Composition of Foods, Agriculture Handbook No. 8*, Agricultural Research Service, United States Department of Agriculture, 1963. Certain domestic vegetables are listed for comparison with wild plants.

A recommended daily allowance (RDA) is considered to be the amount of any vitamin or mineral that is necessary to maintain a healthy body on a daily basis.

The RDA's listed here were set by the Food and Nutrition Board of the National Academy of Sciences—National Research Council. The allowances are higher than the least amounts required for health. The RDA's are subject to change (up or down) as new information becomes available.

RDA's for Adult Men & Women

	men	women
protein	70 grams	58 grams
calcium	800 to 1,400 mg.	800 to 1,400 mg.
iron	10 mg.	18 mg.
vitamin A	5,000 I.U.	5,000 I.U.
thiamine (vitamin B₁)	1.4 mg.	1.0 mg.
riboflavin (vitamin B₂)	1.6 mg.	1.6 mg.
niacin (vitamin B₃)	18 mg.	13 mg.
ascorbic acid (vitamin C)	45 mg.	45 mg.

Most figures are higher for pregnant and lactating women. Also, figures may vary for children according to age and weight.

Measure for vitamin A is given in international units (I.U.).

1 gram = 1000 milligrams (mg.)
100 grams = 3.57 ounces

The quantity of any plant, listed on the following nutritional charts, needed to supply the necessary recommended daily allowance is determined by the following formula:

$$\frac{\text{RDA}}{\text{amount of vitamin or mineral supplied in 100 grams (3.57 oz.) of selected plant.}} \times 100 \text{ grams} = \text{answer in grams}$$

or

3.57 ounces = answer in ounces

Examples:

1. How much dandelion greens do I have to eat to provide my recommended daily allowance of calcium?

$$\frac{800 \text{ milligrams (from RDA's)}}{187 \text{ milligrams (taken from nutritional analysis chart for edible wild plants)}} \times 100 \text{ grams} = 427.80 \text{ grams}$$

or

3.57 ounces = 15.27 ounces of dandelion greens, raw

2. How much watercress do I have to eat to provide my recommended daily allowance of vitamin C?

$$\frac{45 \text{ milligrams (from RDA's)}}{79 \text{ milligrams (from nutritional analysis chart)}} \times 100 \text{ grams} = 56.96 \text{ grams}$$

or

3.57 ounces = 1.99 ounces of watercress, raw

3. How much poke do I have to eat to provide me with my recommended daily allowance of vitamin A?

$$\frac{5{,}000 \text{ International Units (from RDA chart)}}{8{,}700 \text{ International Units (from nutritional analysis chart)}} \times 100 \text{ grams} = 57.44 \text{ grams}$$

or

3.57 ounces = 2.05 ounces of poke, cooked

Vitamin A

The RDA for vitamin A can be met by including yellow and/or green, leafy vegetables in the diet every day. The RDA of vitamin A is 5,000 I.U. for adults. 5,000 I.U. can be provided by one of the following:

1.24 oz. (35.71 gm.) of dandelion greens, raw
2.13 oz. (60.97 gm.) of violet leaves, raw
1.49 oz. (42.73 gm.) of dandelion greens, cooked
1.50 oz. (43.10 gm.) of lamb's quarters, raw
1.59 oz. (45.45 gm.) of carrots, raw
1.98 oz. (56.80 gm.) of sweet potatoes, raw
1.80 oz. (51.54 gm.) of lamb's quarters, cooked

Vitamin C

The RDA of vitamin C for adults is 45 mg. The RDA of vitamin C can be provided by any one of the following:

.74 oz. (21.42 gm.) of violet leaves, raw
.84 oz. (24.19 gm.) of kale, raw
1.13 oz. (32.37 gm.) of turnip greens, raw
2.38 oz. (68.18 gm.) of persimmons (native), raw
2.66 oz. (76.27 gm.) of strawberries, raw
3.15 oz. (90.00 gm.) of oranges, raw, peeled
4.14 oz. (118.42 gm.) of grapefruit, raw

There is some controversy concerning the accurate RDA of vitamin C. "According to Dr. Linus C. Pauling (Nobel Laureate Professor of Chemistry, University of California, Stanford), the optimum daily intake of vitamin C for most adults is from 2,300 to 9,000 mg. Toxicity symptoms usually do not occur with high intakes of vitamin C, because the body simply discharges whatever it cannot use." (*Nutrition Almanac*, Nutrition Search, Inc., by John D. Kirschmann, McGraw-Hill Book Co., 1979.) For more important vitamin C information see page 123, Rose Hips.

Calcium

"Milk is the best source. It is almost impossible to supply the amounts of calcium that are recommended unless milk in some form is used daily and cheese and other milk products are eaten frequently." (*Food, The Yearbook of Agriculture, 1959,* United States Department of Agriculture.) I'm very surprised at this statement, since there are so many green, leafy vegetables, domestic and wild, that provide much higher concentrations of calcium.

The RDA of calcium is 800 mg. for adults. 800 mg. of calcium can be provided by any one of the following:

    9.03 oz. (258.89 gm.) of lamb's quarters, raw
  10.85 oz. (310.07 gm.) of lamb's quarters, cooked
  11.11 oz. (317.46 gm.) of bird's rape, raw
  11.24 oz. (321.28 gm.) of kale, raw
  11.38 oz. (325.20 gm.) of turnip greens, raw
  23.93 oz. (683.76 gm.) of whole milk, 3.7% fat

Iron

The RDA of iron for adults is 10 mg. for men and 18 mg. for women. The following quantities of wild and domestic vegetables provide the RDA of iron.

	men	women
Shepherd's purse, raw:		
	7.29 oz. (208.33 gm.)	13.12 oz. (375.00 gm.)
Purslane, raw:		
	9.99 oz. (285.71 gm.)	17.99 oz. (514.28 gm.)
Jerusalem artichokes, raw:		
	10.29 oz. (294.11 gm.)	18.52 oz. (529.41 gm.)
Beet greens, raw:		
	10.66 oz. (303.03 gm.)	19.09 oz. (545.45 gm.)
Swiss chard, raw:		
	10.93 oz. (312.50 gm.)	19.68 oz. (562.50 gm.)
Dandelion greens or spinach, raw:		
	11.29 oz. (322.58 gm.)	20.32 oz. (580.64 gm.)

Edible Wild Plant Nutritional Analysis Chart

(data based on 100 gram samples)

	calories	protein grams	carbohydrates grams	fiber gm.	calcium mg.	phosphorus mg.	iron mg.	vitamin A I.U.	thiamine mg.	riboflavin mg.	niacin mg.	vit. C mg.
violet greens, raw								8,200				210
dandelion greens, raw	45	2.7	9.2	1.6	187	66	3.1	14,000	.19	.26		35
dandelion greens, cooked	33	2.0	6.4	1.3	140	42	1.8	11,000	.13	.16		18
purslane, stems & leaves, raw	21	1.7	3.8	.9	103	39	3.5	2,500	.03	.10	.5	25
purslane, stems & leaves, cooked	15	1.2	2.8	.8	86	24	1.2	2,100	.02	.06	.4	12
lamb's quarters, raw	43	4.2	7.3	2.1	309	72	1.2	11,600	.16	.44	1.2	80
lamb's quarters, cooked	32	3.2	5.0	1.8	258	45	.7	9,700	.10	.26	.9	37
garden cress (*Lepidium* sp.), raw	32	2.6	5.5	1.1	81	76	1.3	9,300	.08	.26	1.0	69
garden cress, cooked, short time	23	1.9	3.8	.9	61	48	.8	7,700	.06	.16	.8	34
garden cress, cooked, long time	22	1.8	3.6	.9	58	44	.7	7,000	.04	.15	.7	23
watercress, raw	19	2.2	3.0	.7	151	54	1.7	4,900	.08	.16	.9	79
mustard greens (*Brassica* sp.), raw	23	2.2			138	32	1.8	5,800	.80	.14	.6	48
bird's rape (*Brassica rapa*)	32	3.6			252	62	3.0	1,355	.12	.29	1.1	118
shepherd's purse, raw	33	4.2			208	86	4.8	1,554	.25	.17	.4	36
poke, raw*	23	2.6	3.7		53	44	1.7	8,700	.08	.33	1.2	136
poke, cooked	20	2.3	3.1		53	33	1.2	8,700	.07	.25	1.1	82
day lily buds, raw*	42	2.0			87	176	1.2	3,000	.16	.21	.08	88
stinging nettles, raw*	65	5.5						6,500				
mint (*Mentha* sp.), raw	32	3.0			194	48	3.8	1,296	.13	.16	.7	64
Jerusalem artichokes, raw	7	2.3	16.7	.8	14	78	3.4	20	.20	.06	1.3	4

* These plants should be thoroughly cooked before eaten.

Domestic Vegetable Nutritional Analysis Chart

(data based on 100 gram samples)

	calories	protein grams	carbohydrate grams	fiber gm.	calcium mg.	phosphorus mg.	iron mg.	vitamin A I.U.	thiamine mg.	riboflavin mg.	niacin mg.	vit. C mg.
beet greens, raw	24	2.2	4.6	1.3	119	40	3.3	6,100	.10	.22	.4	30
beet greens, cooked	18	1.7	3.3	1.1	99	25	1.9	5,100	.07	.15	.3	15
broccoli, raw	32	3.6	5.9	1.5	103	78	1.1	2,500	.10	.23	.9	113
broccoli, spears, cooked	26	3.1	4.5	1.5	88	62	.8	2,500	.09	.20	.8	90
carrots, raw	42	1.1	9.7	1.0	37	36	.7	11,000	.06	.05	.6	8
carrots, cooked	31	.9	7.1	1.0	33	31	.6	10,500	.05	.05	.5	6
swiss chard, raw	25	2.4	4.6	.8	88	39	3.2	6,500	.06	.17	.5	32
swiss chard, cooked	18	1.8	3.3	.7	73	24	1.8	5,400	.04	.11	.4	16
kale, leaves w/o stems, raw	53	6.0	9.0		249	93	2.7	10,000	.16	.26	2.1	186
kale, cooked	39	4.5	6.1		187	58	1.6	8,300	.10	.18	1.6	93
lettuce (head), raw	13	.9	2.9	.5	20	22	.5	330	.06	.06	.3	6
lettuce (leaf), raw	18	1.3	3.5	.7	68	25	1.4	1,900	.05	.08	.4	18
spinach, raw	26	3.2	4.3	.6	93	51	3.1	8,100	.10	.20	.6	51
spinach, cooked	23	3.0	3.6	.6	93	38	2.2	8,100	.07	.14	.5	28
turnip greens, raw	28	3.0	5.0	.8	246	58	1.8	7,600	.21	.39	.8	139
turnip greens, cooked	20	2.2	3.6	.7	184	37	1.1	6,300	.15	.24	.6	69
potato, baked in skin	93	2.6	21.1	.6	9	65	.7	trace	.10	.04	1.7	20
sweet potato, raw	114	1.7	26.3	.7	32	47	.7	8,800	.10	.06	.6	21
sweet potato, baked in skin	141	2.1	32.5	.9	40	58	.9	8,100	.09	.07	.7	22
New Zealand spinach, raw	19	2.2	3.1	.7	58	46	2.6	4,300	.04	.17	.6	30
New Zealand spinach, cooked	13	1.7	2.1	.6	48	28	1.5	3,600	.03	.10	.5	14
cabbage, raw	24	1.3	5.4	.8	49	29	.4	130	.05	.05	.3	47
cabbage, cooked	20	1.1	4.3	.8	44	20	.4	130	.04	.04	.3	33

Edible Wild & Domestic Fruit Nutritional Analysis Chart

(data based on 100 gram samples)

	calories	protein grams	carbohydrates grams	fiber gm.	calcium mg.	phosphorus mg.	iron mg.	vitamin A I.U.	thiamine mg.	riboflavin mg.	niacin mg.	vit. C mg.
blackberries, raw	58	1.2	12.9	4.1	32	19	.9	200	.03	.04	.4	21
blueberries, raw	62	.7	15.3	1.5	15	13	1.0	100	.03	.06	.5	14
cranberries, raw	46	.4	10.8	1.4	14	10	.5	40	.03	.02	.1	11
elderberries, raw	72	2.6	16.4	7.0	38	28	1.6	600	.07	.06	.5	36
persimmons, native, raw	127	.8	33.5	1.5	27	26	2.5					66
raspberries, raw	73	1.5	15.7	5.1	30	22	.9	trace	.03	.09	.9	18
strawberries, raw	37	.7	8.4	1.3	21	21	1.0	60	.03	.07	.6	59
apples, unpeeled, raw	58	.2	14.5	1.0	7	10	.3	90	.03	.02	.1	4
grapefruit, raw	41	.5	10.6	.2	16	16	.4	80	.04	.02	.2	38
oranges, peeled, raw	49	1.0	12.2	.5	41	20	.4	200	.10	.04	.4	50
bananas, raw	85	1.1	22.2	.5	8	26	.7	190	.05	.06	.7	10
cherries, sour, raw	58	1.2	14.3	.2	22	19	.4	1,000	.05	.06	.4	10
cherries, sweet, raw	70	1.3	17.4	.4	22	19	.4	110	.05	.06	.4	10
peaches, yellow fleshed, raw	38	.6	9.7	.6	9	19	.5	1,330	.02	.05	1.0	7
pears, raw	61	.7	15.3	1.4	8	11	.3	20	.02	.04	.1	4
grapes, raw	69	1.3	15.7	.6	16	12	.4	100	.05	.03	.3	4

Dandelion
Taraxacum officinale

Dandelion

To the *botanist*, it is *Taraxacum officinale*.

To the *entomologist*, it's the host for at least ten common insects.

To the *chemist*, it's the need to invent a better chemical for its eradication.

To the *engineer*, it's a need to invent a more efficient sprayer, as well as being a beautifully engineered parachute design.

To the *geographer*, it can be a good migratory indicator.

To the *gardener*, it's a bothersome weed in the carrot patch, but a fairly good pasture plant.

To the *chef,* it's a pot herb of unique quality.

And to the young *child,* it's a thing of beauty and magic. It's a whistle, it's a bracelet, it's a necklace, it's a yellow powder puff. Its white seed head is a magical package of fairy dancers that can carry dreams and wishes up into the sky. And around the world when launched into a breeze with a kiss blown in love and prayer.

To the *dandelion* itself, it is merely a helpful being, filling in wherever there is a need for a green plant with beautiful flowers and nectar for bees. It loves to be helpful and demands no more than common soil and water.

Ask yourself again—What is a Dandelion? What is a rose? What is a tree? What are you?

By David Lofgren

The common name for this wild food plant, most frequently used in the United States, comes from the French "dent de lion," meaning tooth of a lion because of the saw tooth shape of the leaf margin. To most folks, the dandelion, which spatters with yellow lawns that are expected to stay green, is just not that much of a dandy fellow. Aside from poison ivy, the dandelion may be the most despised of all plants. Not because of a rash it can cause, or some rank odor—it doesn't even irritate any of our five basic senses. But it does irritate many people's sense of pride. People manicure and fondle their lawns until they are a uniform shade of green, just the right thickness and just the right height—really very "unnatural." Now let something natural take place such as the germination of a dandelion seed and the resulting plant . . . then watch the fur fly . . . a declaration of war . . . poisons, trowels, electric shock, whatever it takes to defeat the enemy.

The dandelion has come a long way in the attitudes most people have for it. There has been a complete turnabout from great respect to the present animosity. The scientific name

Taraxacum officinale, identifies the dandelion as the most valuable plant in the wild food and medicinal plant group. Early settlers into the United States brought the dandelion along as a medicine to cure *whatever ailed them.* The English meaning of *Taraxacum officinale* is "the official remedy for disorders," and there is much validity to this. The most common physical disorders of the time stemmed from malnutrition. Old herbals list eye disorders, scurvy, scrofula, eczema, and all eruptions on the surface of the body as being problems all curable by eating the dandelion. This may sound a bit far-fetched and "too good to be true" . . . but it is true.

Listen to this! According to *Compostion of Foods—Book No. 8,* put out by the Department of Agriculture, the dandelion is higher in vitamin A than any other plant. That includes all the vegetables you find in the supermarket. It is also an excellent source of vitamin C, calcium, and other essential nutrients. The presence of all this good stuff can cure a goodly number of ailments stemming from malnutrition.

The amount of vitamin A in a dandelion is phenomenal. An adult needs 5,000 I.U. (international units) of vitamin A per day. One hundred grams of dandelion greens supplies 14,000 I.U. For comparison, raw carrots supply 11,000 I.U., kale 10,000 I.U., and raw sweet potatoes 8,000 I.U., all per 100 grams.

Dandelion has 187 milligrams of calcium per 100 grams of raw greens. Milk, one of our most common sources of calcium, has 118 milligrams of calcium per 100 grams.

One argument I hear from folks who refuse to change their life-styles enough to include dandelions in their diet is this: "I can get my daily requirement of vitamin A from carrots or other supermarket vegetables—so why bother with dandelions?" Three good reasons for bothering with them are: 1. They are as fresh a source of vitamin A as you'll ever get; if you want to you can eat them within seconds of harvest. 2. They cost less than supermarket foods. Compare the price of dandelions in your backyard with the carrots at the nearest grocery store (include gas costs to and from the store). 3. You can get a bonus from supermarket produce that you don't get with dandelions—pesticide residues.

My most memorable recollections of the dandelion are associated with near fatal cases of spring fever. Fatal in the sense that my school grades would suffer near irreparable damage. I remember sitting in algebra class on a hot day, the sun shining, window open and a faint breeze blowing in— then it happened—a "blow away" was caught up in the breeze and found its way into the room through the window. All the class material the teacher was presenting was hopelessly lost as my mind concentrated on the "blow away," seemingly motionless, yet magically moving through the air. I've yet to see a child whose attention couldn't be excited by the seed of a spent dandelion being "blown away" by a gust of wind. The intrinsic value of a dandelion is priceless.

Many people are already familiar with the dandelion's edibility. But what a lot of folks don't know is that besides being a wild food plant, it is also considered a domestic vegetable. Anybody wishing to do so can pick up a vegetable seed catalog such as Burpee's and order dandelion seeds for planting in the backyard vegetable garden. A dandelion sold through a seed company might be expected to have some desirable attributes such as larger leaves, less bitter taste, a tendency to flower later; so it is really a good deal for an individual focusing on nutrition.

What do we do with the dandelion once we have gathered our bagful? The leaves can be the main ingredient in a salad. Use only leaves from areas where the dandelions are growing free from sources of auto pollution that might settle on the plants. I have more than enough growing as weeds in my vegetable garden. Do not use dandelions from along roadsides, as lead oxides and other pollutants may be present. Leaves from lawns that are constantly mowed tend to be tough. Plants with flowers or flower buds have leaves that can be very bitter.

After you have eaten your salad try cooked dandelion greens. The leaves can be prepared as you would any other green, leafy vegetable. Sometimes we have them at home with a cream sauce, or oil and vinegar, or butter, or even like wilted lettuce—dandelions are great with bacon drippings poured over them; but if you are really concerned with health and nutrition, you probably won't eat them this way. It's really tough for a lot of us to bridle our taste buds.

My favorite part of the dandelion is the "crown," the small, tender, white section where the root and leaves join together.

Dandelion Crown Salad

2 cups dandelion crowns
½ cup onions or ramps, diced
¼ head shredded lettuce
2 hard boiled eggs, diced

Mix all ingredients together and add your favorite salad dressing, or try Two-Leaved Toothwort Dressing (page 54).

This is an excellent salad. Try it, you won't be disappointed. The leaves are not the only edible part of the dandelion. As a coffee substitute, the dandelion is often said to be better than chickory.

Dandelion Coffee

Gather some dandelion root and scrub clean. Slice root into 1 inch sections. Roast them in the oven until they snap when broken and are a dark brown inside. Grind and use as you would coffee.

You won't have any trouble finding enough of the root. The dandelion is so difficult to eradicate from lawns because of its large, long root that can sometimes go down as far as 3 feet. I don't have a taste for coffee, whether it is from dandelion or the real thing; you'll have to test it for yourself.

The young roots can also be sautéed in butter and eaten just as is. To me, when prepared this way, they taste like buttered popcorn. Now if you want to go out and collect the roots because you like buttered popcorn—don't—just pop some popcorn and butter it, it's much easier.

The flowers can also be eaten. I'm not too excited about the taste of the flowers, but the best recipe I've tried for cooking the flowers is this:

Fried Dandelion Heads

1 cup dandelion flower heads
1 egg
½ cup wheat germ

Beat the egg thoroughly. Mix the dandelion flower heads completely and equally with the egg. Put the wheat germ in a plastic bag and add a few flowers at a time. Shake so flower heads become coated with wheat germ. Fry or deep fry until golden brown.

One word of warning! Always use a lid when frying with butter. I'm often collecting wild plants, especially mushrooms, to experiment with different recipes. Anytime I fried the plants, the butter in the pan would seem to disappear into thin air; and I would add more butter, then more butter. I would always end up with a meal so rich with butter that after eating a small amount I'd feel bloated. What happens is that part of the butter evaporates and the rest is absorbed into the food being prepared, leaving no liquid for cooking. A lid on the pot will solve this dilemma and save money in butter and energy. More dandelion recipes:

Dandelion Salad

4 cups young dandelion leaves
2 hard boiled eggs, diced
4 strips bacon, diced

Wash, dry and chill dandelion leaves. Dice bacon, fry, drain and mix into leaves. Sprinkle diced hard boiled eggs over the dandelion leaves. Add Peppergrass Oil and Vinegar Dressing (page 54). Toss and serve.

Creamed Dandelion Crowns On Biscuits

2 cups dandelion crowns, diced
1 cup onions or ramps, diced
2 tablespoons butter
2 tablespoons flour
1 cup milk
salt and pepper
paprika

Melt the butter in a saucepan. Add flour and stir over a low heat until mixed. Add milk. Bring to a boil, stirring constantly. Continue stirring and cook to desired thickness. Add the dandelion crowns and the onions, stir and keep warm over a low heat for 3 minutes. Serve hot over biscuits. Add salt, pepper and paprika to taste.

Quick Biscuits

2 cups flour
3 teaspoons baking powder
1 cup milk
¼ cup cooking oil

Heat oven to 450°. Combine all the dry ingredients. Add the liquid ingredients and stir till blended. Drop by teaspoonfuls onto a lightly greased baking sheet. Bake 10—12 minutes or until golden brown. Makes about 16 biscuits.

Dandelion-Ramp Quiche

2 tablespoons butter
1 cup fresh ramps, diced
3 cups fresh, chopped dandelion leaves
4 eggs
¼ teaspoon nutmeg
1½ cups cream
one 9 or 10 inch pastry shell, unbaked
½ cup of grated Swiss or cheddar cheese

Sauté ramps and dandelion leaves in the butter for 5 minutes. Mix, in a blender, the eggs and nutmeg. Scald the cream and add to the blender along with the ramps and dandelions. Purée in the blender. Pour into the pastry shell and sprinkle with grated cheese. Bake at 375° for 20 to 25 minutes.

Creamed Dandelions & Carrots

2 cups chopped dandelion leaves
1 cup carrots, diced (potatoes can be substituted)
2 tablespoons butter
½ teaspoon salt
¼ teaspoon pepper
½ teaspoon sage
1 tablespoon flour
¼ teaspoon sugar
½ cup milk

Boil dandelion leaves and carrots for 5 minutes, then drain. In a skillet, melt the butter. Add the dandelion leaves and carrots, cover with a lid and sauté over a low heat for 5 minutes. Remove from heat and add the salt, pepper, sage, flour and sugar. Mix well, then add the milk. Return the skillet to the heat and bring to a boil, stirring constantly. Lower heat and simmer for 15 minutes. Serve hot.

Wilted Dandelion Leaves

3 cups washed dandelion leaves
3 slices cooked bacon, diced
¼ cup vinegar
2 teaspoons sugar

Fry the bacon until crisp. Add vinegar to the skillet and heat. Remove from heat, add sugar and dandelion leaves, then toss till the leaves are wilted.

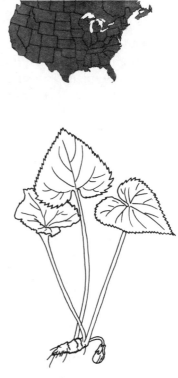

Striped White Violet
Viola striata

Blue Violet
Viola papilionacea

Violets

Margaret Wolfe Hungerford wrote: "Beauty is in the eye of the beholder."[1] I believe that taste is also in that category, but in the mouth of the taster. Often the foods that excite your taste buds just don't do a thing for the next person. Violets are like that. Although I have never run into anyone who disliked the taste of violets, it's somewhere between "they're great" or "they're all right." Of all the plants suitable for a main ingredient in a salad, the violet is probably liked by the most people.

Besides their agreeable taste, violets have quite a few other attributes as a wild food plant. They are one of the most common wild plants. Since conservation is the first consideration one should make before collecting any plant, the violet (because of its wide availability) can be at the top of your foraging list. Here in West Virginia, where I do my foraging, we have 39 plants in the genus *Viola*. Some of these are downright "super plentiful" just about everywhere I look.

The most common species is *Viola papilionacea* or the common blue violet. *Papilionacea* is Latin for butterfly-like. A violet flower does have the basic shape of a butterfly.

I can remember picking large bouquets of blue violets for Mom's table and being rewarded with a big kiss. And after the blue violet season was almost past, the white violets would begin to flower. I would also be allowed to pick the white violets because of their abundance. But let a yellow violet find its way into a bouquet of blue and white violets and . . . I'd better watch out. We were always told that "you shouldn't pick the yellow ones because they're very rare." I've found out since that it doesn't hurt to pick any violet flowers. The showy, butterfly-like flowers, to which most of us are attracted, are the first to appear in the spring. What most folks don't know is that these flowers rarely produce any seeds; therefore, they have very little value in reproduction and can be picked without any harm to the plant itself. This bit of information is valuable to parents and children who have an affinity towards picking pretty flower bouquets. The flowers that maintain the violet's reproductive cycle are said to be "cleistogamous," a 50¢ word which means the flowers never open but bear abundant seeds. These self-pollinating flowers are most often produced during the late summer, close to the ground where the plant emerges from the root stalk. You really have to look closely to see them.

Violets are not only common; they are also easy to identify. Most people are already familiar with the butterfly-like flowers and heart-shaped leaves. Many violet species take their name from the shape of the leaves, such as: Triangle leaf, arrow leaf, three parted, lance leaf and bird foot. Keep in mind that those that have leaves other than heart-shaped should not be collected because of their limited range. Leaves from the yellow violet should never be collected, whether the leaves are heart-shaped or not. They are just not that common. There is also some controversy as to whether or not certain yellow species may be mildly poisonous. Some reliable reports show that certain folks exhibit a strong cathartic reaction.

Now for the information your body wants to know. Like certain other wild plants, violets are a "nutritional treasure house." A ½ cup serving of violet leaves will give you the vitamin C of four oranges and also more than the recommended daily requirement of vitamin A.[2] Violet blossoms are three times as rich in vitamin C, weight for weight, as oranges. Just ½ cup of the greens in your salad gives your body what it needs, saves you some money; and you've eaten some really "natural" food, free of pesticides and additives. Maybe you've enjoyed a walk with your family too.

Now don't make the mistake of thinking that the violet green is a wild food available only in the spring. I've gone out in the dead of winter, swept the snow away with a broom, and collected my four oranges' worth of vitamin C and daily vitamin A. The only difficulty with collecting in cold-cold weather is what you might call the "crystal effect." The frozen violet greens crack and break like crystal, and you end up with nothing large enough to bring home. Handle your greens with kid gloves, let them thaw inside, then put them in your salad. You will be surprised at what is available on a year-round basis.

Here is what you can do with the violet leaves and flowers you collect. First of all, if you can, serve them raw in a salad.

Violet Leaf & Flower Tossed Salad

1 pound fresh tomatoes, quartered
1 cucumber 6—8 inches long, sliced thin
3 hard boiled eggs, diced
4 cups fresh violet leaves
1 cup violet flowers, stems removed

Mix all the above ingredients together and add your favorite salad dressing or try Peppergrass Oil and Vinegar Dressing (see page 54).

Any type of cooking will reduce the nutritive values. Even if your salads come from domestic vegetables and not wild plants, the addition of the right amount of violet leaves will add needed nutrition without changing the taste. The leaves can also be cooked as you would other leafy green vegetables. The leaves are still commonly used to thicken soups and are often called "wild okra."

One of the most imaginative and rewarding things we have ever done with violets is this:

Violet Jello
one 6 oz. box black cherry jello
1½ to 2 cups violet flowers

Combine jello with water according to package directions and pour into a 9"x13" pan. Chill until the jello *just* begins to thicken. Remove the jello from the refrigerator and with your index finger press violet flowers (one at a time) into the thickened surface of the jello until all flowers are embedded. Arrange the flowers side by side until the surface of the jello is covered. Chill jello until firm.

My kids go wild over violet jello. They look forward to it, even ask for it, and best of all they sit still and listen to me tell them about the vitamins, the beauty and whatever else I want to tell them about violets. It's kind of a shady way to get your kids to listen to the important things they normally won't sit still for. But it works.

Over the years violets have been used extensively as a medicinal plant for many ailments. Violets are still listed in the pharmacopoeias (book listing drugs, with description of their properties, preparation and use) of the United States and Great Britian but you may not find the name violet there. Instead you will find names of drugs that contain chemicals that can be extracted from violets. The drug companies go even one step further—they can synthesize the same chemicals that we take in when we eat certain medically valuable, edible wild plants. Millions of violets and other plants are saved each year because it is now possible to duplicate the chemicial properties of these plants. At one time, many people had great faith in "Syrop Violae" (Syrup of Violets). It is listed as a mild laxative and as a cure for ague, epilepsy, inflamation of the eyes, sleeplessness, pleurisy, jaundice and quinsy, to name a few.[3] A lack of vitamin A or C, or both, could cause or aggravate some of the preceeding conditions; so evidently violets are, as Euell Gibbons called them, "Nature's Vitamin Pill.[4]"

Culpepper's old herbal, written in the 17th century, states:

> It is a fine pleasing plant of Venus, of a mild nature and no way hurtful. All the violets are cold and moist, while they are fresh and green, and are used to cool any heat or distemperature of the body, either inwardly or outwardly, as the inflammation of the eyes, to drink the decoction of the leaves and flowers made with water or wine, or to apply them poulticewise to the grieved places; it likewise easeth pains in the head caused through want of sleep, or any pains arising of heat if applied in the same manner or with oil of Roses. A drachm weight of the dried leaves or flowers of violets, but the leaves more strongly, doth purge the body of choleric humours and assuageth the heat if taken in a draught of wine or other drink; the powder of the purple leaves of the flowers only picked and dried and drank in water helps the quinsy and the falling sickness in children, especially at the beginning of

the disease. It is also good for jaundice. The flowers of the violets ripen and dissolve swellings. The herbs or flowers while they are fresh or the flowers that are dry are effectual in the pleurisy and all diseases of the lungs. The green leaves are used with other herbs to make plasters and poultices for inflammation and swellings and to ease all pains whatsoever, arising of heat for the piles, being fried with yolk of egg and applied thereto.[5]

Now that you know the violet, you can make a healthful addition to your salad, have fun with your children and add a great big bouquet of flowers to your table without any guilt feelings for picking them.

More violet recipes:

Candied Violet Flowers

*Candied violet flowers add a beautiful touch
to birthday cakes and other pastries.*

1 quart unbruised violet flowers, stems removed
2 egg whites, slightly beaten
1 cup granulated sugar

Dip the violet flowers in water. Dry gently. Carefully and thoroughly brush the egg white onto the flower petals using a small fine-hair paint brush. Sprinkle the flowers, tops and bottoms, with sugar. Spread out on wax paper and allow to dry.

Violet Hors d'oeuvres

8oz. package cream cheese
¼ lb. corned beef or chipped ham, finely chopped
1½—2 tablespoons dark or light mustard (let your
    taste buds decide)
1 cup violet flowers, stems removed
whole violet leaves

Blend cream cheese, corned beef and mustard together. Roll into 1 inch balls and flatten slightly. Cover completely with violet flowers. Chill and serve on whole violet leaves.

Violet Jelly

2 cups violet blossoms
juice from 1 lemon
1 package powdered pectin
4 cups sugar

Rinse the violet flowers in cold water. Put the flowers in a quart jar and cover with boiling water. Screw on the lid and let them sit for 24 hours. After 24 hours, strain out 2 cups of the liquid. Add the lemon juice, the powdered pectin, and bring the mixture to a boil. Add the sugar, boil again and boil hard for 1 minute. Pour into ½ pint jars and seal.

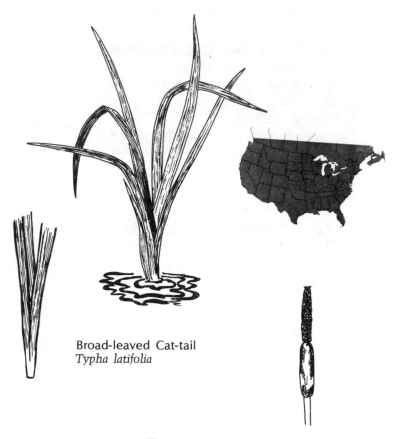

Broad-leaved Cat-tail
Typha latifolia

The Cat-tail

"Let nature be your teacher," said William Shakespeare. There is more truth to that saying than you might believe. This chapter on cat-tails, like the other chapters in this book, is aimed at "wetting your whistle" enough to get you outside to see and sample these plants first hand. The paragraphs that follow won't teach you *all* about cat-tails; cat-tails teach you all about cat-tails. I can give some facts and personal experiences, but your own experience is what's going to "turn you on" to cat-tails as a wild food.

Cat-tails have taught me a lot. As a boy, my weekends were spent with my father at a favorite fishing haunt in Butler County, Pennsylvania. One end of the lake provided the water source: A stream, slowly meandering through a large cat-tail swamp. My fondest memories of cat-tails have nothing to do with their edibility but with such things as the fierce territorial defenses of the red-winged blackbird, muskrat lodges and the spawning grounds of the large-mouthed bass. Wild foods will save money and provide much needed nutrition, but so much more is in store for anyone who stops long enough to look and listen to what the cat-tails are saying: "Adopt the pace of nature, her secret is patience." (Emerson actually.)

The common cat-tail *(Typha latifolia)* is one of the best wild food plants for beginners. Identification is easy, and it grows throughout the United States and in many other countries. If there are streams, swamps, or wet areas where it doesn't grow, it can be easily introduced. Introduction of the cat-tail into vast areas of the "Third World" countries is being seriously considered. It grows on land previously thought useless and may be a large part of the answer to solving the world's food shortage.

I collect cat-tails along streams, around edges of farm ponds, and along—believe it or not—interstate highways in West Virginia, Ohio and Pennsylvania. Next time you are on an interstate, check for cat-tails; but make sure you get permission from the State Police or Highway Patrol before you start picking. Believe me, State Highway Patrolmen are not very understanding when cat-tails are used as an excuse for parking along the berm of the highway. After all, the signs do say "Emergency Parking Only," and cat-tails are hardly considered an emergency, at least not by supermarket-shopping policemen.

Eating cat-tails is not a new idea. The ancient Chinese and Egyptian civilizations esteemed the cat-tail as a food and fiber plant. And the Cossacks of Russia have long considered the cat-tail a delicacy, hence the name "Cossack asparagus." Collect the plants in the spring when they are two to three feet tall; cut them off at or just below water level (it depends on how clean the water is). Peel back the outer green, then whitish-green plant material until you get to the pure white, tender, center section. The taste is somewhere between a cucumber and a watermelon. No other wild food plant matches the flavor and tenderness of the "Cossack asparagus." What you don't put in your salad bowl you can boil and serve as you would asparagus.

Cossack Asparagus Over Turkey & Biscuits

16 Cossack asparagus sections, 4 inches long
4 slices cooked turkey or turkey loaf, each about six
    inches square
cheese sauce (see recipe below)
biscuits (see Quick Biscuit recipe on page 27)

Boil the Cossack asparagus sections in ½ gallon of water for 5 minutes. Put 4 biscuits in each of 4 bowls. Place 1 slice of turkey over the biscuits in each bowl. Drain the Cossack asparagus sections, put 4 on each slice of turkey and cover with cheese sauce. Serves 4.

Cheese Sauce

2 tablespoons flour
2 tablespoons butter
1 cup milk
¼ teaspoon dry mustard
½ cup shredded cheddar cheese

Melt butter in a small sauce pan then add flour. Cook until it's blended and bubbly. Add milk and stir until it's thick and creamy. Add dry mustard and cheese and cook, stirring constantly, until cheese is melted and blended. Makes 1¼ cups.

Cossack asparagus is truly a delicious addition to the supper table. I have never had anyone turn their nose up at it once they have tried it; cooked or raw in a salad.

As spring turns into summer the cat-tail produces the beginnings of a flower spike; still green and wrapped in a papery-like sheath. This spike is often referred to as "cat-tail corn" due to its taste and the character of its construction.

Cat-tail Corn

8 green flower spikes
1 quart water
4 tablespoons butter
Parmesan cheese

Cut the green flower spikes off one inch below the spike itself, remove the papery sheath and boil in the water for 5 minutes. Drain water, add butter and lightly sprinkle with Parmesan cheese. Serve and eat as you would corn on the cob.

The taste is similar to corn. After you have eaten those tender, green flower buds from the spike, discard the hard center section as you would the cob from an ear of corn. Keep in mind that as and after the flower spikes turn brown they become inedible. You wouldn't be poisoned if you accidently ate one, but you probably would just as soon chow down on a bowl full of cotton. Think green! I have also prepared the cat-tail spikes in the following way.

Scalloped Cat-tails

6 green cat-tail spikes
1 quart water
1 egg, beaten
¼ cup melted butter
pinch of nutmeg
¼ teaspoon pepper
½ cup milk
¼ cup grated cheese (your favorite)
2 tablespoons butter

Drop the cat-tails into a quart of boiling water and boil for 4 minutes. Drain and cool. Scrape off enough flowers (the soft, green portion) to make about 1¼ cups. Place in a bowl; add the egg, butter, nutmeg and pepper. Mix well. Scald the milk and add slowly to the cat-tail mixture. Mix well again. Pour into a buttered baking dish, sprinkle with grated cheese and bake at 375° for 30 minutes. Come and get it while it's hot!

Shortly after the green spikes turn to a light brown, a brilliant gold appears as the pollen-laden flowers blossom. My first experience with this pollen was very mysterious. I was crossing the previously mentioned cat-tail swamp to reach a favorite fishing spot. While I was watching my footsteps, the pollen-laden flowers were gently swatting my face, arms and clothing. By the time I was through the swamp, I was the most beautiful golden-yellow spatter print you'd ever seen. The mystery was that I had no idea what the "yellow-stuff" was or where it had come from. It was at least an hour before I figured where the yellow powder originated. Well, it was some ten years later that I learned about the edibility of the "yellow-stuff." Shake the pollen from the flowers into a plastic bag, mix half and half with regular flour and bake to your heart's content. Once you see the warm, yellow color of your first loaf of cat-tail pollen bread, you'll be making cat-tail cookies, cat-tail pancakes, cat-tail everything. As for nutrition, certain pollens have been found to be very high in protein, and the cat-tail is probably no exception. The yellow color hints at a high vitamin A content.[6]

If that is not enough from the cat-tail, it has one more use as a wild food plant up its sheath. The root can be recycled (by peeling, drying and grinding) into an all purpose flour. Use as you would regular wheat flour or mix it half and half.

More cat-tail recipes!

Cat-tail Root Biscuits

1 cup cat-tail flour
1 cup wheat flour
3 teaspoons baking powder
1 cup milk
¼ cup cooking oil

Collect the cat-tail roots. Wash, then remove and discard fibrous outer peel. Dry the roots for 2 hours in an oven at 250°. After baking, pulverize the root and put it through a flour sifter to remove any remaining fibers. Preheat oven to 450°. Combine cat-tail flour, wheat flour and baking powder. Add the liquid ingredients and stir until blended. Drop by spoonfuls onto a lightly greased baking sheet. Bake 10—12 minutes or until golden brown. Makes approximately 16 biscuits.

Cat-tail & Chickweed Salad

1 cup white, tender, cat-tail stem centers
2 cups chickweed leaves
½ cup diced, mild cheddar cheese
your favorite salad dressing

Slice the cat-tail stems into ½ inch sections, mix in the chickweed leaves and cheese. Top with your favorite dressing.

Cat-tails Au Gratin

¾ lb. white, tender, cat-tail stem centers
1 tablespoon butter
1 hard boiled egg
1 pint white sauce (see recipe below)
½ cup sharp cheddar cheese
½ cup bread crumbs

Cut the cat-tails into 1 inch sections and cook in boiling water for 5 minutes. Melt the butter in a baking dish, drain the cat-tails and spread evenly in the baking dish. Grate the hard boiled egg into 1 pint of white sauce and pour over the cat-tails. Sprinkle with cheese and bread crumbs and brown in a broiler.

White Sauce

2 tablespoons flour
2 tablespoons butter
1 cup milk

Melt the butter then add the flour. Cook until blended and bubbly. Add milk and stir until thick and creamy. Makes 1 cup of white sauce.

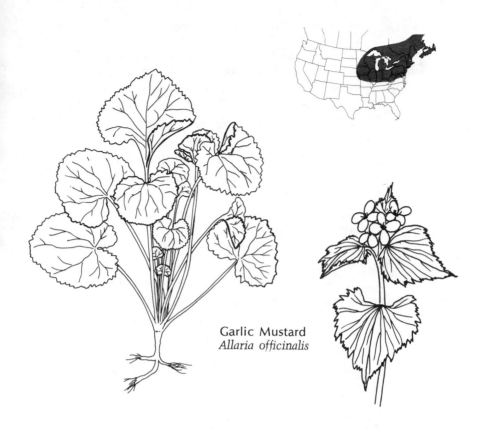

Garlic Mustard
Allaria officinalis

The Mustards

Mustards were somewhat of a stumbling block for me in my plant taxonomy class. Knowing the meaning of words such as silique, silicle and tetradynamous are essential to identifying the mustards, but for some reason my mind wouldn't accept these complicated-sounding words. I could memorize the definitions of the words for a test, but they were soon forgotten or confused. There are two ways that my mind seems to remember such confusing terms. One way is through repetition. I teach certain natural history topics over and over again. The repetitiveness of parts of these workshops templates in my mind the facts and ideas I'm relating to the participants. The second way is through what I like to call "a practical focal point." It was through this means that I learned the mustard family characteristics. Identification for the sake of identification seemed very impractical to me (although I'm hooked on keying plants—it's fun). However, when I was introduced to the wild food qualities and nutritional attributes of the mustards, I became intensely interested in their identification. I now have a practical focal point with the mustards. Identification for the sake of putting a name to a plant is no longer my goal, but identification for the sake of nutrition and taste really excites me. Identifying mustards for the sake of nutrition is, to me, very practical. The mustard's wild food qualities are my focal point.

Now for those confusing words essential to the identification of the mustards:

1. Cruciferae—This is the Latin family name for the mustards. Crucifer, meaning cross, refers to the flower shape. Always four petals making a cross.

2. Tetradynamous—A 50¢ word for six stamens— four long and two short.

3. Silique—A long, slender fruit of certain mustard genera.

4. Silicle—a short, broad fruit of other mustard genera. (All mustards have one of these two fruits: Silique or silicle.)

If you are a health food enthusiast you will want to eat the wild mustards raw in order to capture the total vitamin content—an excellent supply of vitamins A, B₁, B₂, and C. In my opinion, most mustards are slightly bitter when eaten raw. But with such a storehouse of vitamins, I can put up with the bitterness and add them to a salad anyway.

The mustard family is represented throughout most of North America by several edible plant species. If you can gather garlic mustard *(Allaria officinalis)*, you won't have to contend with the bitter taste. With its mild garlic flavor and a profound lack of bitterness that is found among its relatives, garlic mustard could easily be considered the gourmet treat of the wild mustards. According to *Gray's Manual of Botany,* garlic mustard is found along roadsides, in open woods and near habitations from Quebec and Ontario, south to Virginia, Kentucky and northeast Kansas. What a delightful addition to a salad! Get to know this plant; and if it's not in your area, collect some specimens elsewhere (where it's common) and transplant it nearby. You won't regret the effort.

Of all the mustards, those in the genus *Cardamine* are the most sought after for salads. Purple cress *(Cardamine douglassi),* bulbous cress *(Cardamine bulbosa),* cuckoo flower *(Cardamine pratensis),* Pennsylvania bittercress *(Cardamine pensylvanica)* and mountain watercress *(Cardamine rotundifolia)* represent this genus as being edible. There are twelve species in this genus, all which may be edible (none are known to be poisonous), but the five mentioned are the only ones I have eaten or know of that are regularly eaten. Purple cress grows along streams in most of the deep ravines near my home. The leaves are small and it appears that it will take forever to gather enough of them for a meal. But this plant is so abundant that it is not long at all before you are on your way back home with a bag full of nutrients. Bulbous cress has a peppery taste and can be used as you would horseradish.

The other three Cardamines are mildly pungent and among the most delicious of all the wild salad plants. Near my home in West Virginia, mountain watercress is very common and totally overlooked. I have virtually no competition for this plant and can collect all I can eat in a very short time. Just as common is Pennsylvania bittercress which has long been considered an excellent substitute for the European water-cress. Cuckoo flower is reported for West Virginia by *Gray's Manual,* but we have no specimens in our state herbarium. I have yet to taste this plant, but *A Field Guide to Edible Wild Plants* by Lee Peterson assures me that it is well worth the wait. The cuckoo flower is found in swamps, springs, wet meadows and wet woods from northern Canada south to Minnesota, northern Illinois, northern Ohio and northern New Jersey.

Black mustard *(Brassica nigra),* charlock *(Brassica kaber),* and bird's rape *(Brassica rapa)* are probably—not justifiably but

Purple Cress
Cardamine douglassi

Bulbous Cress
Cardamine bulbosa
same as Purple Cress
except flower color and root stalk size

Pennsylvania Bittercress
Cardamine pensylvanica

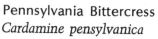

Cuckoo Flower
Cardamine pratensis
same as Pennsylvania Bittercress
except larger flower

probably—the best known and considered the best tasting mustard greens. They are good, but let taste be your guide and try the mustards yet to be mentioned before you decide what your favorite may be.

The Brassicas should be collected when young, in the early spring. As they mature the bitterness intensifies. Prepare as you would any other cooked green, then season to taste. I prefer a little butter or an oil and vinegar dressing.

Yellow rocket or winter cress *(Barbarea vulgaris)* and spring cress *(Barbarea verna)* are the most common mustards where I do my foraging. They both grow as a prolific weed in fallow farm fields and are often a sight to behold. Several acres of the yellow mustard flowers waving on a windy day are beautiful to me, although I know a number of farmers who curse these plants at least once a week. The young leaves are an excellent addition to a salad, and they are great when cooked like spinach. Once you become acquainted with these two plants, you will soon become familiar with the characteristic rosette growth of the young leaves. Collect the leaves from this rosette *before* flower stalks begin to appear.

European watercress *(Nasturtium officinale)* has been named by the late Euell Gibbons as the "King of Wild Salad Plants."[7] It is grown throughout Europe and in the United States as a domestic food plant, yet it can be found growing wild in all our 50 states. Many folks don't realize that watercress is in the mustard family. I have seen it on restaurant menus and in markets and often wondered why it costs so much. I used to think, since it tastes so good in a soup, on a sandwich, or in a salad, and because it comes all the way from Europe, it has to be expensive. But to my surprise, it grows wild near my home. The only place I have encountered watercress is in running water; and unfortunately, the water hasn't always been very clean. If you have any doubt as to the water quality where you collect your watercress, either discard it, cook it thoroughly and use it as a cooked green (it's excellent cooked), or soak it in water in which a water purifying tablet such as halazone has been dissolved.

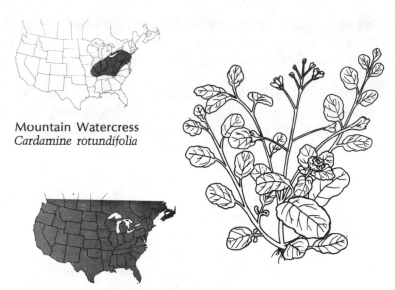

Mountain Watercress
Cardamine rotundifolia

European Watercress
Nasturtium officinale
(no illustration)

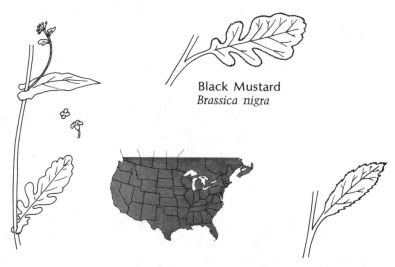

Black Mustard
Brassica nigra

Bird's Rape
Brassica rapa

Charlock
Brassica kaber

When collecting watercress, never collect the whole plant no matter how tempted you may be. Pinch the plant off where it emerges from the water, and the rootstock will continue supplying you with new foliage throughout the year. If you cannot locate watercress, order as much seed as you think you will need and seed those streams. It won't be long before you have more watercress than you can handle.

Besides in a salad or as a cooked green, try this recipe.

Watercress Soup

2½ cups watercress leaves, chopped
6 cups chicken stock
1 clove garlic, crushed
1 teaspoon parsley flakes
pinch of sage
salt and pepper to taste
3 egg yolks

Place all ingredients, except the egg yolks, in a large saucepan. Bring to a boil, then simmer for 30 minutes. Remove the garlic. Beat the egg yolks; add them gradually to the soup while stirring rapidly. Simmer very slowly for another 10 minutes.

One of my favorite sandwiches consists of a pile of watercress leaves mixed with a thick layer of cream cheese between two slices of whole wheat bread. Not much different from those fancy, little, expensive watercress sandwiches for weight-conscious socialites—except that my sandwich is twice as large and about one-eighth the price. What's the moral to this bit of information? Never buy something you can get for free. Remember, this book is to be used as a guide to economy as well as nutrition. You will save at least $1.50 on each watercress sandwich you make yourself. Once you have become addicted to the taste of watercress, you will discover new ways to tickle your taste buds.

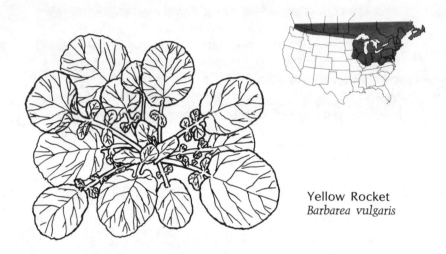

Yellow Rocket
Barbarea vulgaris

Shepherd's Purse
Capsella bursa-pastoris

(no illustration)

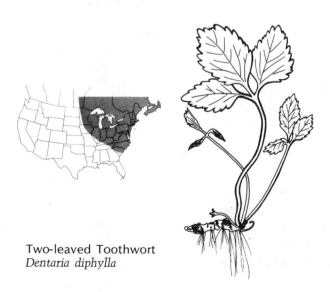

Two-leaved Toothwort
Dentaria diphylla

Two-leaved toothwort *(Dentaria diphylla)* is the "garnish mustard." The rootstock of this mustard is large and pungent. It is horseradish-like, yet different. Grated and sprinkled over a salad it makes a delightful garnish. Grated and mixed with a French dressing, mayonnaise or whatever, this mustard becomes a salad dressing.

If that's not enough, try Shepherd's purse *(Capsella bursa-pastoris)* or field pennycress *(Thlaspi arvense)*, or one of the peppergrasses *(Lepidium* sp.), or another mustard plant you may discover to be edible. You don't know what you're missing until you've tried them all.

More mustard recipes follow.

Bulbous Cress Dressing

1 cup bulbous cress (leaves or rootstocks)
2 cups salad dressing
½ cup water

Chop the bulbous cress leaves or rootstocks as finely as possible. Put the salad dressing, water and bulbous cress in a blender and purée.

Tomato—Cardamine Spread Sandwich

4 slices of bread
1 medium tomato, thinly sliced
4 ounces cream cheese
2 tablespoons salad dressing
½ cup cardamine leaves (any species), diced

Blend the cream cheese, salad dressing and cardamine leaves. Spread on 2 slices of toast. Cover with tomatoes and other slice of toast. Makes 2 sandwiches.

Hamburger Stew with Mustard Seasoning

1 pound hamburger
2 medium potatoes, diced
3 carrots, sliced
1 onion (medium)
1 can cooked tomatoes
1 cup green beans or peas
1 cup cardamine leaves (any species)
1 tablespoon minced two-leaved toothwort root
1 teaspoon chopped peppergrass leaves
salt and pepper to taste

Brown the hamburger. Add the raw vegetables and tomatoes including the cardamine leaves and toothwort root. Simmer until the vegetables are tender. Add the peppergrass leaves, stir and let sit for 5 minutes. Reheat if necessary. Serve hot.

Shepherd's Purse Potatoes

4 baking potatoes
1 cup Shepherd's purse (leaves, stems & seedpods)
½ cup grated cheese (your favorite)
2 tablespoons butter

Bake the potatoes until they are soft throughout. Slice potato skins open on one side. Remove the potato with a spoon and save the skins. Boil the Shepherd's purse in 1 quart of water for 5 mintues. Drain and add the Shepherd's purse and butter to the potatoes and beat with an electric mixer. Put the mashed potato and Shepherd's purse mixture into the potato skins, sprinkle with cheese and bake at 250° until the cheese is melted. Serves 4.

Cream of Mustard Soup

4 tablespoons butter
2 tablespoons flour
3 cups milk
1 cup black mustard, charlock or bird's rape,
    chopped, (leaves only)
2 beef bouillon cubes
salt and pepper to taste

Put butter, flour, 2 cups of milk, mustard leaves and bouillon cubes in a blender. Blend for 10 seconds. Pour into saucepan and add the remaining cup of milk. Let simmer for 5 minutes but do not boil. Salt and pepper to desired taste.

Two-Leaved Toothwort Gravy

1 cup chicken or beef bouillon*
1 teaspoon sugar
2 to 3 tablespoons two-leaved toothwort root
1½ to 2 tablespoons flour
1 tablespoon butter
salt and pepper to taste

Add the toothwort root, flour, and butter to the bouillon. Boil 15 to 20 minutes, stirring constantly. Add the sugar and salt and pepper to taste. Serve over potatoes or stuffing.

*Make bouillon by dissolving a bouillon cube in 1 cup of water.

Two-Leaved Toothwort Dressing

1 cup two-leaved toothwort root
2 cups salad dressing
½ cup water

Put the toothwort root and water into a blender and purée. Add salad dressing and blend.

Two-Leaved Toothwort Seafood Dip

1 cup two-leaved toothwort root
1½ cup catsup
½ cup salad dressing

Purée the toothwort root and salad dressing in a blender. Add catsup and blend again.

Peppergrass Oil & Vinegar Dressing

2 tablespoons salad oil
2 tablespoons vinegar
fresh peppergrass, to taste

Shake oil and vinegar together until mixed. Add fresh peppergrass (finely chopped) and mix again.

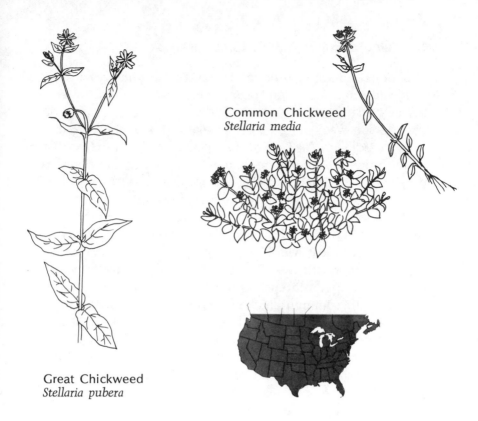

Common Chickweed
Stellaria media

Great Chickweed
Stellaria pubera

Chickweed

Chickweed gets its name from the great enthusiasm that chickens and small birds have for this plant. If you keep an eye on your garden in the spring and fall when there is not much gardening activity, you will notice flocks of chipping sparrows and other birds plopping themselves down to a feast of chickweed.

Anytime a person takes an interest in wild food plants, a certain risk factor is involved. Poisonings from foraging for edible wild plants are rather rare, but a number of people do become totally turned against edible wild plants because they were a bit too quick to "pick a name" for what they mis-identified as something good to eat. I believe that chickweed doesn't have the popularity it deserves because of negative experiences due to misidentification. To me chickweed is the *best* wild salad ingredient. Comments have passed my ears such as "that stuff is terrible" or "I'd rather eat _____." Maybe that person was eating _____ thinking it was chickweed.

According to *The Flora of West Virginia* (this is the text that I use for identification), the name "chickweed" can apply to nine different plants representing five genera of plant groupings. And the difference between the taste and texture of the chickweed is from good to bad to ugly. The chickweed referred to in wild food guides and herbals is *Stelleria media.* It is one of our most widespread plant species. Being circumpolar, common chickweed is found in North America, South America, Europe, Asia, and elsewhere. Most early sailors were familiar with common chickweed because one of the most prevalent ailments amongst these sailors was scurvy. At that time, no one knew the cause of scurvy, but they knew a cure—chickweed. Common chickweed was the miracle drug of the time, at least for the men of the sea. Without fresh fruit or vegetables for months at a time while aboard ship, scurvy (caused by lack of vitamin C) was widespread in the crew. With the advent of glass blowing, a method of avoiding scurvy was discovered: Growing fresh greens in "bottle gardens." One of the first recorded uses of what we now call terrariums was for keeping a fresh supply of chickweed and other medicinal plants at hand.

During the early spring and fall, common chickweed is the dominant weed in many gardens and grows thick enough for many, many salads. But if you are like me and get a bit frustrated picking those tiny leaves, your mind wanders searching for an easier way. And after you have picked and picked it looks like you have very little for your effort, well don't fret, there is a solution. In my many visits to the woods, meadows, and streams around my home, I began to develop a mental picture of the flora, especially the plants that can be used in salads. Areas that are not quite swamps, but are still very damp most of the year and somewhat shaded, hold another chickweed, *Stellaria pubera,* called great chickweed.

The leaves of the great chickweed are three to four times as large as in the common chickweed, saving 45 minutes out of every hour spent picking the smaller chickweed. I pick only the leaves, but the stems can also be used as salad material.

More chickweed enters my stomach than any other wild food save certain berries and mushrooms. On excursions through the woods, whether bird-watching or botanizing, whatever, I purposely go near one of my great chickweed patches where I can sit down and snack between meals. Just like so many other wild food salad greens, chickweed can be chomped on all-year-around. Flowers appear January through December. I can remember the first time I brushed the snow away to collect chickweed and found those little, white, star-like flowers. It was an exciting moment for me.

Eat your chickweed raw. You need the vitamin C. Euell Gibbons' *Stalking the Healthful Herbs* makes reference to a green drink made by liquefying chickweed in a blender along with a number of other assorted herbs, wild and domestic.[8]

Charles Pierpoint Johnson writes, in *Useful Plants of Great Britian,* "It forms when boiled an excellent green vegetable much resembling spinach in flavor and is very wholesome."[9]

On the medicinal scene, common chickweed has been held in great repute among herbalists as an ointment. The fresh leaves and stems are used as a poultice on swollen areas and open sores, with very satisfying results. As Gerard tells us (Gerard, John. *Herball.* London, 1633.) in one of the older herbals:

> The leaves of Chickweed boyled in water very soft, adding thereto some hog's grease, the powder of Fenugreeke and Linseed, and a few roots of Marsh Mallows, and stamped to the forme of Cataplasme or pultesse, taketh away the swelling of the legs or any other part . . . in a word it comforeth, digesteth defendeth and suppurateth very notably."[10]

Don't take chickweed lightly. Look for it, you'll find it. Some chickweed recipes follow.

Chickweed-Pea Salad

4 cups chickweed leaves
2 cups raw peas
1 small onion, minced
4 ounces cheddar or Swiss cheese, sliced in thin
    strips
6 tablespoons mayonnaise
2 teaspoons sugar
2 slices bacon, crisp and crumbled

In a large bowl place half of the chickweed, peas, onion, and cheese. Sprinkle with 1 teaspoon of sugar. Dot with 3 tablespoons of mayonnaise. Repeat layers. Cover and refrigerate for 1 to 2 hours. Add bacon and toss just before serving.

Chickweed & Mustard Greens

1 quart chickweed (leaves & stems)
½ quart mustard greens—*Brassica* or *Barbarea* (one
    of the more pungent mustards is recommended
    but any can be used)
1 ramp, diced (a small onion can be substituted)
2 tablespoons butter
salt
½ cup bacon pieces or grated cheese

Boil the mustard greens in 2 quarts of water for 10 minutes. Add the chickweed and boil for 2 more minutes. Drain and chop the greens. Mix in the diced ramp or onion. Season with salt and butter. Sprinkle with bacon pieces or grated cheese.

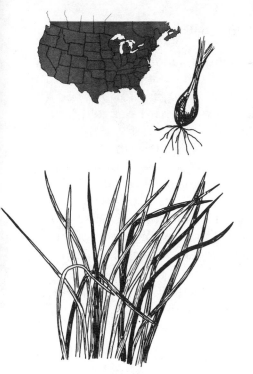

Wild Meadow Garlic
Allium canadense

The Ramp
Allium tricoccum

The Ramp

Thus far we have dandelions, violets, cat-tails, mustards and chickweed for our salad. How about an onion? The ramp is a wild onion sometimes referred to as a wild leek, and it is in a class by itself among the edible wild plants.

The domesticated leek has been highly esteemed for quite some time with gourmet cooks, since the flavor blends so delicately with other foods. Now, if those gourmet cooks were the outdoor type and took to grubbing around in the woods every now and then, the ramp would be about as scarce as hen's teeth. Fortunately, this is not the case. Ramps are plentiful in many areas, contrary to popular belief. I run into thousands of ramps in the woods around my home, yet I hear people speak of how the ramp is a mountain plant and "aren't nowhere near here." I shared these beliefs for quite awhile—until I identified my first ramp. I had just been ignoring this common plant because of what I was told. You can't believe everything you hear.

Ramps are so popular in West Virginia that several communities hold annual "ramp festivals." These festivals are attended by two kinds of folks: Them that like ramps and them that don't like ramps who have heard those "nasty" ramp stories. The ramp festivals are springtime events, and anyone interested can get dates, locations, and other information from the Department of Natural Resources, Charleston, West Virginia.

Oh yes . . . there are "nasty" ramp stories. If you shy away from onions because they leave your breath less than appealing, go on to the next chapter, ramps aren't for you. It is said that the folks living downwind within several miles of the ramp festivals can't hide from the odor (their property value has hit rock bottom since the first ramp festivals), the paint curls and peels in the kitchens where the ramps are cleaned and cooked, and there are different classrooms in the schools for them that did and them that didn't.

When I eat ramps I encourage my wife to do likewise. The very first time I ate these delicacies I quit counting at eleven. My wife, Bev, moaned and groaned about the lingering aroma for three entire days. I brushed my teeth, gargled mouthwash, bathed—all to no avail. And I honestly convinced myself that Bev was carrying this joke a little too far, until I arrived at work. The first person I talked to asked, "Have you been eating ramps?" You sometimes have to take the good with the bad.

Ramps *(Allium tricoccum)* are wild onions. Like all onions and garlic they are in the genus *Allium.* The mention of wild onions is often accompanied by the response, "Oh, I know what they are." But they aren't. The tall, thin, grass-like clumps that appear in winter and persist through summer and smell like onions aren't onions at all. They are one of the wild garlics, probably crow garlic *(Allium vineale)* or meadow garlic *(Allium canadense)*, found in cow pastures, lawns, meadows and places where people are likely to encounter them. Such an injustice to confuse these *Alliums* with the ramp. Ramps are broad-leaved, just as are domestic leeks. They look like small leeks.

If you cannot find any ramps in the woods near home, or if they are down right scarce and for conservation reasons you dare not dig any, then take a lesson from J.A. Chapman. As I mentioned in the chapter on mustards, watercress can be seeded into clean streams: Ramps can be seeded into damp deciduous woods. But unlike watercress, ramp seeds cannot be bought through a garden seed catalogue. The seeds must be collected from the wild.

Here is what I do. I search out new ramp patches. Here in West Virginia, April 14 is what I call "ramp day." At this time of year ramps are nearly full grown, the leaves are bright green, and they are taller than other spring plants still pushing through the soil. They are very obvious. Second, I mark the location of the ramp patches. I am careful to mark the exact location. By the first day of summer the ramps have all but disappeared. The leaves have withered, fallen off and are mostly decayed. Only the root (which you can't see) persists. A very slender flower stalk soon appears, and by mid-October an abundance of seeds are present. Third, after the first real hard frost (about 20°F), I visit my ramp patch. I look for the slender, brown stalks and collect the jet black seeds attached all along, midway to the tip of the stalk. Last, I do with my ramp seeds as J.A. Chapman did with his apple trees in the early spring, or even better, in late winter if possible.

Ramps are great in a salad or raw with spaghetti (I like them with spaghetti), but I pay the price. Anytime that ramps are eaten raw your newly acquired odor will be a faithful companion for the next 2 to 3 days. However, once they are cooked, their effect on how well you "win friends and influence people" is about the same as with ordinary super-market onions.

Most of the ramps we eat are cooked a very special way.

Bev resented ramp season until she was coerced into her first bowl of ramp soup. Now it is not uncommon for her to make ramp soup three or four times a week during the season.

Ramp Soup

1 cup ramps (leaves & bulbs)
1 tablespoon butter
2½ cups water or 2 cups milk and ½ cup water
2 bouillon cubes (beef or chicken)

Clean and dice the ramps. Add butter to a soup pan, add the ramps and sauté over a very low heat (remember to use a lid). Add the water or milk and the 2 bouillon cubes. Simmer for 15 minutes.

Now you have ramp soup. But what really makes it worthwhile is this little added effort. Toast 1 piece of bread per bowl of soup. Float a piece of toast in each soup bowl, sprinkle with your favorite cheese, then set the bowls in a hot oven until the cheese is melted. All I can say is: Bev, a "skeptical" wild foods enthusiast, loves it.

If you run into an abundance of ramps and have had all the ramp soup you care for, try this recipe:

Pickled Ramps[11]

Use ramps as large as onion sets. Detach the green stems and leaves (remember to save them for your salad) and the root hairs. Wash the bulbs and cook them in water until you have a rolling boil. Drain and pack in small jars.

Make pickling solution by combining:
1 cup water
1 cup vinegar
sugar to taste
pinch of salt

Bring to a hard boil and pour over the hot ramps. Put on lids and process in a pressure canner for 5 minutes at 5 pounds pressure.

Do bear in mind that there are other *Alliums*. They are good in salads, soups, wherever you can make use of onions. And remember to look for them in late winter through spring. If you have trouble finding them, use your nose. Break a couple of the tall, thin, grass-like leaves—the characteristic odor is unmistakable.

More ramp recipes follow:

Ramp Hors d'oeuvres

10 pickled ramps
2 to 3 slices bread
1 tablespoon butter
1 teaspoon bacon pieces

Mix the butter and bacon pieces and spread evenly over the bread. Wrap each ramp in just enough bread to completely cover. Slice in half, chill and serve.

Ramps, Potatoes
and Scrambled Eggs

5 ramps, diced (leaves and bulbs)
4 medium potatoes
2 eggs
3 tablespoons butter

Slice the potatoes thin (do not remove the skins). Melt the butter in a skillet and add the potatoes and ramps. Cook over a medium heat. Use a spatula to stir and turn frequently. When the potatoes are tender add the eggs and stir and turn until eggs are cooked (approximately 2 minutes).

Ramp-Vegetable Pie

1 to 1½ cups corn
2 medium potatoes, diced
3 carrots, sliced crosswise
6 ramps (bulbs & leaves), diced
1 pepper, minced
1 cup peas
2 bouillon cubes

Prepare pie dough for a 2-crust pie, roll and fit half crust into pie pan. Cook the vegetables and bouillon cubes with enough water to cover. Cook until vegetables are tender. When tender, add 1 to 2 tablespoons of flour or enough flour to make broth slightly thick. Pour the vegetable combination with the thickened broth into the unbaked pie shell. Cover with the second crust, seal and bake 35 to 40 minutes or until the crust is a golden brown at 425°. If desired, sprinkle with ½ cup of shredded cheddar cheese before adding the top crust.

Ramp & Rice Soup

5 ramps (tops & bulbs), diced
½ cup rice
½ cup milk
1 teaspoon minced parsley
½ cup Swiss cheese, grated
2 eggs
1½ teaspoons flour
salt and pepper to taste

In a saucepan, in 2 quarts of water, boil the ramps and rice until the rice is soft. Mix the flour and milk together and add it to the saucepan. Beat the eggs and slowly add them to the saucepan, stirring constantly. Serve sprinkled with cheese and parsley. Salt and pepper to taste.

Ramp Gravy

1 teaspoon butter
2 ramps (tops and bulbs), diced
1 tablespoon flour
1 tablespoon vinegar
2 cubes chicken or beef bouillon dissolved in
    2 cups water
salt & pepper to taste

In a saucepan over low heat, place butter and ramps. Cook until the ramps are browned. Stir in the flour, add the bouillon, vinegar, and salt and pepper to taste. Cook for 10 minutes. Serve over mashed potatoes.

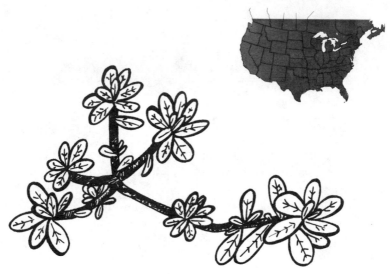

Purslane
Portulaca oleracea

Purslane

Purslane *(Portulaca oleracea)*, sometimes called pussley, is very common in most parts of the United States and southern Canada. Look for it in rich, cultivated soil and waste places; few gardens are without it. The species name *oleracea*, is Latin for "like a garden vegetable." It is probably a weed right among your garden vegetables. Charles Dudley Warner wrote in *My Summer in a Garden:*

> The sort of weed which I most hate is the 'pussley,'
> a fat ground-clinging, spreading, greasy thing and
> the most propagatious plant I know, but I saw a
> Chinaman once boil a lot of it in a pot and stir in egg
> and mix it with relish.[12]

Besides being common and good to eat, it is also easy to identify. It looks like an out-of-place succulent. It grows prostrate with thick, fleshy, reddish-orange stems creeping out in all directions. The leaves are small, green and also very fleshy. Wild stonecrop is the only other plant with which I am familiar that has a succulent-like appearance. I have yet to see wild stonecrop as a weed in cultivated areas, although it is very common in rich, damp woods.

Purslane, like so many other greens, is best when gathered at a young stage, before it is capable of flowering. Telling the young stage from the flowering stage can be difficult since the tiny, yellow flowers open only in "bright" morning sunshine. When the flowers are not open they are locked up tight as a drum, and it takes a very careful eye to notice the flower buds. To keep purslane producing, just collect the leafy tips. These will soon be replaced by new growth. Keep picking the new growth as long as the season lasts. The hardy little purslane plant will produce as often as you pick, with no ill effect to the plant.

Purslane is excellent in a salad. The stem color, leaf shape, and size do wonders for the aesthetics of a salad. To me, the taste is that of a mild oxalic acid; similar to, but much milder than sour grass (also known as European yellow wood sorrel, *(Oxalis europaeo)*. Usually about two weeks before my leaf lettuce is ready to bolt (produce a flower stalk and become bitter), the purslane in my garden makes its first appearance. One of my favorite wild food salads is available at this time.

Purslane & Leaf Lettuce Salad

½ cup purslane
2 cups leaf lettuce
1 hard boiled egg, diced (optional)
your favorite salad dressing

Combine the purslane, leaf lettuce, and egg. Add the salad dressing.

Depending upon your personal preferences this next bit of purslane information will be viewed as a most desirable attribute or a detriment. Purslane has for some time been considered an excellent soup thickener. Like okra, it does wonders to the consistency of a soup or stew. When I first ate it raw I immediately knew why it was a great thickener. It has a thick, somewhat slimy, mucilaginous consistency. It sounds horrible, and to some folks a mouthful of purslane is horrible. I am perfectly comfortable with purslane in a salad, but Bev claims that just the thought of a mouthful of purslane sends chills down her spine.

Purslane can be fried or boiled, and it is great as an addition to a stuffing served with chicken or turkey.

Many folks who are not familiar with purslane's edible qualities view it as nothing more than a troublesome weed. But anyone who has eaten it and doesn't have problems with its consistency knows that it is a truly valuable and beneficial plant.

Purslane Omelet

4 eggs, well beaten
4 tablespoons milk
1 cup purslane
2 tablespoons butter
4 tablespoons grated Swiss cheese

Mix together eggs, milk, and purslane. Melt the butter in a skillet or omelet pan then add the omelet mixture. Use a lid and cook over a very low heat. Never hurry an omelet. Our omelets cook at least ½ hour, usually longer. If you are not using an omelet pan, turn the omelet when the top is still wet but not runny. Add the cheese and turn off the heat. Serve when the cheese is melted.

Purslane & Bread Stuffing

1 loaf homemade bread
1½ cups purslane
1 medium to large onion, diced
3 cups chicken broth (use 1 bouillon cube
    for each cup of water)
3 tablespoons of fresh sage or
    2 tablespoons of dry sage
3 to 4 celery stalks, diced
½ package of dry, chicken noodle soup mix
    (optional)

Combine all ingredients. Wrap in foil or place in a greased baking dish and bake at 350° for 50 to 60 minutes.

Day Lily
Hemerocallus fulva

Day Lily

This is the only common edible wild plant that I sometimes have reservations about eating. It is prolific along roadsides where I live and its flower buds appeal to my taste buds; but it is so beautiful. It doesn't hurt to collect it, but I can't decide whether I want to eat it or put it in a vase. The day lily *(Hemerocallis fulva)* is a stunning wildflower. The flowers are orange lilies up to five inches across, and each plant is capable of producing a dozen or more flowers. If the day lily is used as a flower arrangement, collect a flower stalk with four or more flower buds. The botanical name *Hemerocallis* comes from two Greek words: hermera (a day) and callos (beauty). The flowers are definitely considered beauties; and after expanding for a single day, they collapse and fall off. That is why a bouquet needs to have several flower buds. The buds won't all flower at the same time so at least two days (usually more) of beauty can be received from one flower stalk.

The day lily is native to Eurasia. Since its introduction to the United States, it has spread throughout most of the eastern United States, the mid-west, and southern Canada. I used to think that picking numerous flower buds would deplete or even obliterate the day lilies from an area. Not so; the day lilies growing in the United States rarely produce viable seeds, therefore the flowers have little to do with the proliferation of the plants. Once a plant begins to grow, it rapidly spreads by branching rhizomes and tuberous roots.

The best part of the day lily plant is the flower bud, but it took me a while before I discovered just how good the buds really are. Through my own ignorance, I became alienated toward the day lily as an edible wild food. I was teaching a week long edible wild foods course to a small group of fifth grade students. My main concern was getting the kids excited about wild foods. They were very open to my teaching and willing to try any plants I suggested. Considering the fact that they all came from supermarket-shopping families, I felt very successful. Because of our positive taste experiences with the plants we had eaten throughout the week, the kids had come to trust my edible wild plant information. On the last day we found a large patch of day lilies. I knew the buds were edible but wasn't familiar with their preparation. After my assurances that the day lily buds were good to eat, we "chowed down." Everybody tried the buds. I hadn't realized (I should have known) that the buds should be cooked. Initially they tasted good, but shortly afterward a very uncomfortable feeling invaded our mouths. It wasn't painful, just displeasing, and not at all exciting. All in all we had a successful week, but I was responsible for ending the class on a sour note. The event turned me against the day lily for a full year.

Whatever you do, cook the flower buds. Only three to five minutes of boiling is necessary. Are they delicious! And if ever you tire of day lily buds, which I doubt, reach for new horizons: The day lily tubers are sweet and plentiful. Their nutty flavor makes them great in a salad. Also, the day lily stalks (when about a foot tall) can be boiled for a few minutes and seasoned to your taste. Or the inner portion of the stalk can be eaten raw in a salad.

Some day lily recipes:

Day Lily Salad

1 cup day lily buds, sliced
½ cup day lily tubers, diced
1 tablespoon vinegar
3 tablespoons salad oil
½ teaspoon two-leaved toothwort root, finely
    minced (optional)

Boil the day lily buds for 5 minutes, drain and let cool. Mix in the day lily tubers with the buds. Mix together the vinegar, oil, and toothwort root. Pour over the buds and tubers, mix well, and refrigerate for at least 1 hour before serving.

Day Lily Bud Supreme

1 pound day lily buds sliced in 1-inch sections
1 cup bread crumbs
¼ cup butter
¼ teaspoon savory

Boil the day lily buds for 5 to 10 minutes (until tender), then drain. Melt the butter in a saucepan, and mix in the bread crumbs and savory. Brown over a low heat. Add the day lily buds and mix well. Serve hot.

Day Lily Bud Soup

1 cup day lily buds, chopped
1 pint water
1 cup milk
1 cup cream
1 soup bone
½ cup celery, diced
2 ramps (tops & bulbs) or one small onion, diced
¼ teaspoon thyme

Combine the water, milk, and cream; add the day lily buds and lightly boil for 5 minutes. Add the remaining ingredients, heat to boiling, and simmer for 2½ hours.

Deep Fried Day Lily Buds

3 to 4 cups day lily buds, whole
1 cup flour
1 teaspoon baking powder
½ teaspoon salt
1 egg
1 cup milk
¼ cup salad oil

Combine in a mixing bowl, all the above ingredients, except the day lily buds, and mix well. Heat 3 to 4 inches of cooking oil in a deep fryer or electric fry pan to 375°. Dip the *dry* day lily buds in the batter and deep fry until golden brown.

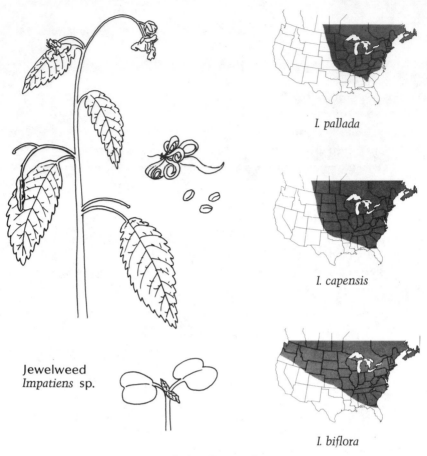

I. pallada

I. capensis

I. biflora

Jewelweed
Impatiens sp.

Jewelweed

Jewelweed, Touch-Me-Not, Impatiens, Speckled Jewels and Quick-In-The-Hand are just a few of the names used throughout the United States to identify this valuable plant. Impatiens is also the name for the cultivated varieties used as ornamental plantings in rock gardens and hanging baskets.

The pale jewelweed or touch-me-not *(Impatiens pallida)* has a pale yellow flower and is sometimes referred to as our woodland species. It is found in moist, shady woods and along streams. The spotted jewelweed *(Impatiens capensis)* has an orange flower mottled with reddish brown and has more of an affinity for sunlight. Look for it in sunny, moist locations, along streams, roadsides and damp meadows. They both flower (at least in West Virginia) from June to October.

Impatiens, the Latin word for impatient, is named for the sudden bursting of the fruit capsules when touched. The comon names touch-me-not and quick-in-the-hand also refer to its seed releasing characteristics. I can remember running through vast areas of the touch-me-nots, bursting the seed capsules, and seeds shooting out in all directions. The first time I realized the mechanism responsible for seed dispersion, I spent most of the rest of that day exploding any swollen capsules I could find. As the seeds mature, the capsules swell and begin to dry; at this stage the slightest agitation can trigger the explosion. But don't let those seeds get away from you. They are dead ringers (by taste) for walnuts. Granted, they are very small; but with the price and availability of walnuts, the seeds are at times worth collecting. And there are usually thousands of touch-me-not plants for every walnut tree you can find. Be careful that the capsules aren't quicker than you are. We often explode them into a plastic bag so as not to lose any seeds, and then separate the seeds from the capsules after we are finished collecting. The seed can be used to flavor puddings, cookies and breads.

Besides the seeds, the jewelweed plant itself makes an excellent wild food. Though several older texts list jewelweed as "possibly" being mildly toxic, the more recent information is quite the contrary. Collect the young sprouts in the spring when they are 4 to 6 inches tall. Cut them into 2-inch lengths, boil them for 10 minutes, drain away the water and season with butter and salt. They are good. You can experiment with them to find other ways you like them prepared. The very young sprouts, about 2 inches tall, are good raw in a salad and jewelweed sprouts in cream sauce on toast makes an excellent breakfast.

My first childhood encounter with the jewelweed was quite accidental. Anytime my friends and I found ourselves near a stream one thing that invariably happened was a leaf-boat race. Each one of us would get hold of a leaf and release it into the water, in the same spot , at the same time. The leaf that first crossed the predetermined finish line farther downstream was the winner. Jewelweed leaves can't get wet, they float on top of the water over every rapid and turbulence in the stream. Leaves from other plant species can't hold a candle to jewelweed leaves. The only other leaf I've found that can give jewelweed a run for its money is lamb's quarters.

The common names jewelweed and speckled jewel result from unwettability of the leaves. When the dew is heavy and the sun is just peeking over the horizon, the water beads up on the leaves. The result is a display of different colored jewels refracting the sun's light into every color of the spectrum—it's a sight to behold.

Jewelweed also has a reputation for being a cure-all for poison ivy, nettle stings and athlete's foot. Since jewelweed and poison ivy grow in approximately the same geographical range and are very often growing together, jewelweed may truly be considered a "jewel of a weed." Anything that can prevent or cure poison ivy is tops in my book.

The recipe for the poison ivy remedy is simple. Take a potful of jewelweed, cover with water and boil it down until the liquid is half its original volume. The strained juice can now be used to prevent a rash after contact has been made with poison ivy or in treating the rash after it has developed. The only difficulty is that the juice will not keep. But don't despair. All you have to do is put the juice into ice cube trays and freeze it. Anytime you come in contact with poison ivy or develop a rash, take a frozen jewelweed cube and let it melt over the affected areas.

Jewelweed is also excellent for treating nettle (itch weed) irritations. Although discomfort from nettles only lasts for 10 to 20 minutes, it can make a person miserable during that time. Take a jewelweed stem, crush it and rub the juice over the itchy area—relief will be immediate.

Anyone who has ever had a bout with athlete's foot—listen carefully. The following quotation is from an article in the book called *Antibiotics That Come From Higher Plants,* as it appeared in *Crops in Peace and War,* the 1950-51 Yearbook of Agriculture published by the U.S. Department of Agriculture.

At the University of Vermont, Thomas Sproston, Jr. and associates tested 73 plant extracts, directing particular attention toward those that show fungicidal or fungistatic properties. The most active antifungal extracts were obtained from *Impatiens* (wild touch-me-not), *Cuscumis melo* (muskmelon) and *Tropeleoleum majus* (nasturtium). The crystalline antifungal agent isolated from *Impatiens* was 2-methoxy-1, 4-napthoquinone.[13]

The frozen jewelweed cubes are as effective for athlete's foot as they are for poison ivy. Get to know the plant. It should be a welcome visitor to your dinner table and medicine cabinet.

Some jewelweed recipes follow.

Creamed Jewelweed Shoots & Rice

1¾ pounds of young jewelweed shoots
    (4 to 6 inches tall)
boiling water
3 tablespoons butter
¼ cup flour
1½ cups milk
1 teaspoon soy sauce
2 hard boiled eggs, diced

Place the jewelweed shoots in a large saucepan. Cover with boiling water and boil for 5 minutes. Drain and cut the shoots into small sections. Melt the butter in a saucepan, stir in the flour, soy sauce and milk. Cook until the sauce thickens. Add jewelweed shoots and the eggs. Serve hot over cooked rice.

Jerusalem Artichoke
Helianthus tuberosus

Jerusalem Artichokes

Such an important sounding edible wild plant. The name
doesn't fit the plant at all. The name Jerusalem is said to be a
corruption of the French word for sunflower, girasol. But it is
not even closely related to the artichoke. A more meaningful
name for this impostor might be potato sunflower. The
portion of the plant that we're interested in collecting is the
tuber, which resembles our domestic potato. And it is a
sunflower. I encourage anyone interested in wild food
foraging to become familiar with some of the Latin and Greek
names of the edible wild plants in this book. With a basic
understanding of these names, valuable insight concerning
the edible, nutritional, and sometimes medicinal qualities of
these plants can be obtained. *Helianthus tuberosus* is the

Jerusalem artichoke's botanical name. *Helianthus* is a combination of two Greek words: Helios (the sun) and anthos (a flower). Tuberosus is Latin for tuberous. That is exactly what it is, a tuberous sunflower.

Jerusalem artichokes can be found growing in rich or damp thickets and along streams from southern Canada to Georgia, Tennessee, and Arkansas. Since it has become so popular as a domestic vegetable, its range is becoming greatly extended. Just about any major vegetable seed company will have the Jerusalem artichoke available for home vegetable gardeners. It is also becoming quite popular in supermarkets. All the major supermarkets in my locale carry Jerusalem artichokes.

At the time of flowering, the Jerusalem artichoke stands from three and a half feet to ten feet in height. Look for groups of plants. There are usually at least a dozen or more of the plants growing close together. The flowers are just like the flowers on our large garden sunflower but much smaller. Each plant bears several to many flowers. Quite a few sunflowers fit this description, so examine the roots. If the rootstocks bear tubers, it is the Jerusalem artichoke. If the rootstocks do not bear any tubers, it is some other wild sunflower; better luck next time. Locate your Jerusalem artichokes when they are in flower, but don't dig them until fall. After locating your first Jerusalem artichokes be prepared for a pleasant surprise. There are bunches and bunches of tubers under those plants. Unlike the potato, the Jerusalem artichoke can be harvested even in the dead of winter, so dig them as needed but don't take them all. Leave a few tubers spaced about three feet apart, and by fall there will be just as many, if not more, as were collected the year before.

I went fishing along a stream near my home and as usual, I became more interested in the plants, birds and other wildlife that were present. I'm not a "sit and wait" fisherman; I'm constantly moving. While I was walking along the stream, I saw about a dozen Jerusalem artichokes. Not the plants, but the tubers. They were lying in my path alongside the stream.

To my left the stream bank was about six feet above the water level, and the top of the bank was covered with sunflowers. During high water the stream would cut into the bank removing the soil and exposing the plant roots. I didn't have to do any digging to identify these sunflowers. Their tubers were hanging everywhere. I collected the exposed tubers and began to undercut the bank myself. The soil would fall, and the tubers would just hang there. It was more like picking apples than collecting Jerusalem artichokes. This particular group of Jerusalem artichokes supplied our family with tubers for two long seasons before the stream finally washed away the plants once and for all. There is no telling how many tubers were washed away, some may be destined to take up residence elsewhere and start a new crop for some other forager to find.

If for some reason you can't find Jerusalem artichokes in the wild, try growing your own. Tubers and planting instructions can be ordered from most seed companies. Provide water on a regular basis, and soon an established Jerusalem artichoke patch will spring up. Once the plants are established, they should need no further attention. Just stand back and watch out. And I do mean watch out. They should be contained, if possible. I advise anyone planning to start Jerusalem artichokes in the garden to dig down below the top soil and bury railroad ties or some equivalent barrier around the perimeter of the Jerusalem artichoke patch. After going through all that work they still may escape into the rest of the garden. If that happens, treat them as any other garden weed. Don't let them become established where they are not wanted.

As far as nutrition, Jerusalem artichokes cannot compare with many of the other wild food plants already mentioned. Although, when compared with domestic vegetables, they make a very good showing. They do have a high starch content but not in the usual carbohydrate form. Instead, the starch is in the form of inulin, making it an excellent food for diabetics or anyone else on a low starch diet.

Jerusalem artichokes can be used in any recipe that calls for potatoes. They can be eaten raw or cooked. If the recipe calls for cooking, use a covered pan over a low heat. Jerusalem artichokes cook much faster than potatoes; therefore *do not overheat*, or they can get tough.

The popularity of the Jerusalem artichoke as an edible wild plant has given way to its ever-growing demand as a regular in many home vegetable gardens.

Jerusalem Artichoke Picnic Salad

¼ cup Italian salad dressing
4 cups Jerusalem artichokes, sliced
1 cup celery, chopped
2 ramps (tops & bulbs), chopped
4 hard boiled eggs, sliced
½ cup mayonnaise
salt and pepper to taste

Boil the Jerusalem artichokes until tender. Pour the Italian salad dressing over the Jerusalem artichokes while they are still warm. Chill for 2 hours. Add the celery, ramps, eggs, and mayonnaise; mix slowly. Chill and serve as a potato salad substitute. Serves 6 to 8.

Jerusalem Artichoke Skillet

¼ pound loose sausage
1 clove garlic
3 cups Jerusalem artichokes, thinly sliced
1½ cups shredded cabbage
2 medium onions, sliced

Fry the sausage in a skillet. Add the garlic, onion, Jerusalem artichokes, and cabbage to the skillet. Add ½ cup of water, cover and cook until the Jerusalem artichokes are tender. Top with ¼ to ½ cup of your favorite shredded cheese.

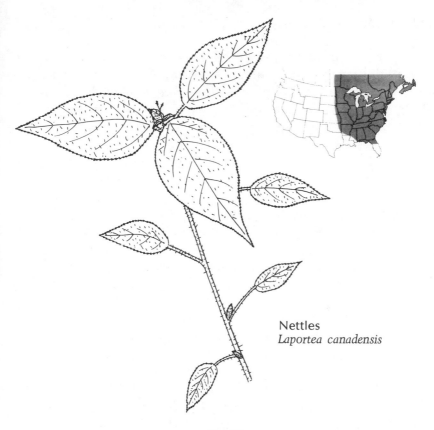

Nettles
Laportea canadensis

Nettles

Who would ever try to eat a nettle? I used to ask myself that question every time I'd see the nettle listed as a wild food plant. To me, nettles are to wild foods what stinkhorns are to edible fungi. Sure they may be edible, but who in the world would try to eat them?

My memories of nettles certainly are not fond ones; almost every weekend I'd have "itchy knee caps" as a boy. When my father and I took our weekend fishing trips, we would have to walk through wooded areas or overgrown fields to get to the most productive "bass holes." My knees were just the right height to hit that old itch-weed. I remember when I bought my first hip-boots, it meant that certain parts of the stream would be more accessible and also, that most of my nettle discomforts would be gone.

The stinging apparatus of the nettle is found all over the top of the leaves, on the veins on the underside of each leaf, and all along the stem. When the tiny, sharp, hollow spines are touched, they puncture the skin and secrete an irritant causing the affected area to welt up and become very itchy.

Certain nettles make excellent potherbs. Wood nettle *(Laportea canadensis)* and stinging nettle *(Urtica dioica)* are the best tasting and most common. Wood nettle ranges from the extreme south of Newfoundland and Quebec to Manitoba, south to Nova Scotia, New England, Florida, Alabama, Mississippi, Missouri and Oklahoma. Look for it in low woods and banks of streams. Stinging nettle is found in waste places and along roadsides from Newfoundland to Manitoba, south to Nova Scotia, New England, Virginia, and Illinois.

I prefer wood nettle over the other nettles. Wood nettle is easy to distinguish since it is the only nettle possessing stinging hairs that has an alternate leaf arrangement. Wood nettle is also quite common in all eastern and most midwestern states.

Collect the tender tops of the wood nettle and the stinging nettle before they bloom. Regardless of which nettle you collect, there are two essential requirements that must be observed between the time of collection and eating. First, wear gloves! You cannot collect any type of "stinging" (some kinds of nettles do not have stinging hairs) nettle without great discomfort unless you wear gloves. And secondly, always cook your nettles before eating them. The stinging quality only disappears with boiling. I doubt if anyone would try to eat nettles raw—but I once told a lady about bedstraw's *(Galium aparine)* reputed value in aiding weight loss. She went home, ate some raw, and ended up with several small, but uncomfortable, scratches on her lips.

Prepare nettles as you would any other cooked green. Nettles lose a great amount of their volume when cooked, so collect much more than you think you'll need. And if you get rewarded by a number of little white welts, remember the jewelweed. It can help relieve your discomfort (see page 76).

Stinging Nettle
Urtica sp.

Delicious Nettles

1 pound fresh nettle greens
2 tablespoons butter
¼ cup light cream
1 level teaspoon prepared horseradish
2 hard boiled eggs, diced

Boil the nettles for 25 minutes; drain and chop. While the nettles are cooking, combine the butter, cream, and horseradish in a small saucepan and cook over a low heat. Pour, all or part of, the sauce over the nettles. Sprinkle with the hard boiled eggs.

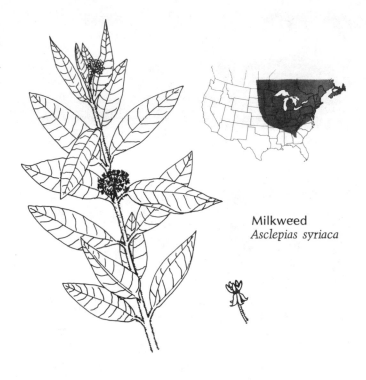

Milkweed
Asclepias syriaca

Milkweed

The common milkweed *(Asclepias syriaca)* is one of the most abundant edible wild plants. It is found in dry soil, fields, and roadsides from southern Canada south to Kansas, Tennessee, and Georgia.

I remember breaking the leaves off the stem and chasing or being chased by one of the neighborhood kids who was trying to "get me" with the sticky, white sap. The first time I heard the plant referred to as milkweed was when someone told me the sap was good for removing warts. At about the same time, my grandmother told me I could rub half of a raw potato over my wart, go outside, throw the potato over the house, and the wart would be gone within a week. Neither person seemed to have much faith in his wart-removing remedy, so I didn't try either one. Herbals still list the milkweed sap as having wart-removing qualities, but I remain a skeptic about this home remedy. Introducing the milkweed as an edible wild food by talking about warts is not very appetizing, but that was how I was first introduced to this plant. Now we can discuss the milkweed's edible qualities.

As the seasons progress and the milkweed plant matures, it provides new uses as an edible wild food. When the milkweed first appears in the spring, it looks very much like asparagus and can be prepared in much the same way. Collect these asparagus-like shoots before they reach eight inches in height. But foragers beware! Indian hemp *(Apocynum cannabinum)*, a poisonous plant, is available at the same time as the young milkweed shoots, is similar in appearance to asparagus, and even has a milky sap. I have never heard of anyone accidentally eating Indian hemp, but just the same, be careful. Don't confuse the two.

Milkweed Au Gratin

1 pound ramps (tops & bulbs), diced
1 cup cooked milkweed asparagus
1 cup mashed potatoes
4 scrambled eggs
1 cup white sauce (see page 42)
grated cheese, your favorite

Line a buttered pie dish with the mashed potatoes. Add the ramps, milkweed asparagus, and scrambled eggs. Cover evenly with the white sauce. Sprinkle with grated cheese. Brown lightly in the broiler. Serve hot.

After the plants get larger and the leaves unfurl, the flower buds are produced. These unopened flowers are called "milkweed broccoli." They look like green balls (the size of tennis balls) composed of many smaller green balls (the size of small peas). If they are gathered while they are still green, boil them for 10 minutes, drain and discard the water, add new water and boil again for five minutes. This process eliminates slight bitterness. I keep a close watch on my milkweed broccoli so I can collect it at the "pinking stage." At this stage it takes on the color of the opened flowers, but it is still in the bud. The trick is to collect it as near to flowering time as possible. If it is picked just before flowering, the extra change of water can be eliminated, most of the bitterness will be gone, and the flower buds will have a special sweetness. This sweetness is the nectar that has been produced for the "grand opening" being planned for all the local insects. Milkweed broccoli is a good domestic broccoli substitute. I have grown broccoli in my garden with great success and also with a great many insects, but the milkweed broccoli is virtually insect-free. I rarely find an insect on the milkweed broccoli; but if there is one present, it is easy to see and shake off.

Milkweed Broccoli Casserole

2 pounds milkweed broccoli (separate the small
  stems with flower buds from the main stem.)
4 eggs, beaten
2 cups cottage cheese
½ cup ramps (tops & bulbs) or onions, diced
1 cup carrots, diced
1 cup cheddar cheese, shredded
¼ cup butter
½ cup bread crumbs
¼ teaspoon sage, chopped
salt and pepper to taste

Put the milkweed broccoli in a greased 11x7x2 inch baking dish. In a large bowl, mix the eggs and cottage cheese well. Add the carrots, ramps or onions, cheddar cheese, sage, and salt and pepper to taste. Melt the butter, mix it with the bread crumbs, and spread evenly over the top of the casserole. Bake at 350° for 45 minutes.

The next stage of the milkweed is the opened flower cluster. All the insects absent from the flower buds can be found on the opened flowers. A bee keeper friend told me that the flowers are often so laden with nectar that the bees get trapped in the sticky mess and never get off. I have never seen a bee stuck on the milkweed flowers, but I have seen many other kinds of insects trapped in this sticky situation. If you don't mind the extra protein, the few attached bugs won't bother you. But if you're like me, you'll make an added effort to rid the milkweed flowers of every last insect. Once the flowers are cleaned, remove them from the stems and add them to a pancake batter.

Milkweed Flower Pancakes

2 cups milkweed flowers (no stems)
1 cup whole wheat flour
1 cup white flour
1 teaspoon baking powder
1 tablespoon sugar
2 cups milk
2 eggs, well beaten
2 tablespoons cooking oil

Add all the dry ingredients to the liquid ingredients and mix well. Add the milkweed flowers. Fry on a hot, greased griddle.

The nectar is super plentiful and sweet and it makes a delicious pancake. But to top it off, the flower not only provides the pancake, but the syrup for the pancake as well.

Milkweed Syrup[14]

6 cups milkweed flowers
1 cup water

Boil the milkweed flowers in 1 cup of water. Cook on a medium heat for 35 minutes. Stir often to help the flower nectar mix with the water. When the syrup begins to thicken, strain into a ½ pint jar and discard the flowers. Refrigerate. Serve on pancakes, waffles, French toast, or toast.

Late in summer keep a watchful eye for the seed pods. About this time the insects have lost interest in the milkweed due to the falling of the flowers. Don't put off collecting the seed pods or they will mature into what I call the "fish stage." At this stage the inside of the pods resembles small fish, scales and all. When the pod reaches the fish stage, it begins to get too tough to eat. Young, hard pods, however make an excellent okra-like vegetable. Slice them as you would okra, and boil in salted water or simmer in a little cooking oil.

I learn a lot about plants that has nothing to do with their edibility. Just being around the milkweed has taught me many things. I am always excited when I see a Monarch, the milkweed butterfly. The Monarch caterpillar feeds on the milkweed plant. When foraging I often encounter the larva and an occasional shiny green, gold-speckled chrysalis. After I have all the edible parts of the milkweed I want, I collect a chrysalis and the leaf to which it is attached, put it in a gallon pickle jar and observe it several times a day. Before long I have the rare opportunity to see something truly amazing: A worm-like caterpillar transformed into a full-fledged butterfly.

The milkweed is considered one of our most versatile plants due to its great variety of people benefits. It has provided me with a greater appreciation of the natural world. I see a special design in all life, but the milkweed exemplifies this special design. The milkweed seed is a miraculous bit of construction: A little seed surrounded by dozens of fine, white hairs with no two hairs touching. It is as if they are all separate yet working together to achieve some common goal. Their flights are their most impressive attribute. Their movements are delicate and fluid, yet they appear motionless as they float up and down. And if caught in a whirlwind, they go round and round as they climb out of sight into the sky. To sit quietly in a meadow on a breezy day as the milkweed is going to seed, and look, listen, and wonder is a spine-tingling experience.

These same fluffy seeds can be used as an insulating material in clothing. Some people refer to it as "milkweed down." Probably it is not as efficient at holding body heat as goose or duck down, but I'm told that it is an acceptable substitute, especially when considering the price of a down jacket or vest. If you decide to try the milkweed down, make sure you collect it at the right time. If you are too early, it will still be wet; and if you are too late, the fluffy seeds will all have blown away. I would rather watch them blow away.

Lamb's Quarters
Chenopodium album

Lamb's Quarters

Lamb's quarters is a weed of cultivated and waste ground found from the Atlantic coast north into Canada, south to Flordia and Texas, and westward.

Lamb's quarters boasts of a handful of names. Some call it pigweed. I'm not sure why it's called that, but I suspect pigs are very fond of it (What don't pigs like?). Others identify it as wild spinach; it is one of the best potherbs. Botanically speaking, the most appropriate name is goosefoot. *Chenopodium album*, the Latin name, means white goosefoot. The leaves have the basic shape of a goose's foot, and the underside of each leaf is covered with granular white dots that easily rub off.

The best place to look for lamb's quarters is growing as a weed in a vegetable garden. Dandelion, chickweed, poke, purslane, and, of course, lamb's quarters are dominant weeds in my garden, therefore much of my foraging can be done in my backyard. In my college days, I asked my landlord's permission to forage in his garden. I said, "May I weed your garden?" He said, "Sure, but why do you want to do that?" I told him I wanted to eat some of the weeds. He didn't say anything else; he just took a long, hard look at me. I wouldn't be surprised if that incident is still a topic for some of his conversations. It's probably not a good idea to ask a perfect stranger for permission to raid his vegetable garden, but there are usually friends or neighbors who wouldn't mind. Remember, eating weeds, to some folks, puts wild food foragers on their list as candidates for the funny farm. There is nothing wrong with foraging for wild plants; it is just that most folks aren't used to the idea.

Lamb's quarters is excellent as a cooked green. It cooks down to ½ its original volume, so always collect twice as much as is needed. The taste is similar to that of spinach, and in certain recipes I prefer it over spinach.

There is a good chance that the first year anyone looks for lamb's quarters they will be somewhat limited as to how much they can collect. Plant identification guides describe the plants according to floral characteristics, and if one waits until lamb's quarters flowers to collect it, it will be too late. It is very important to learn to recognize all wild edible salad greens and potherbs in their early stages of growth. This is when they are at their best as far as taste and tenderness are concerned. Lamb's quarters can grow as tall as five feet, but these larger plants are tough and somewhat bitter. Collect lamb's quarters when they are less than one foot tall and have no flowers. Young plants can be found from approximately April 1 to October 1 in the northern panhandle of West Virginia.

Lamb's quarters is tougher than spinach and is not really suited for salad use. Because of this toughness, these greens should be cooked slightly longer than spinach would be cooked. When properly prepared, lamb's quarters has the taste and tenderness of spinach, is more nutritious than spinach, and can be substituted in any recipe that calls for cooked spinach.

Lamb's Quarters Greens Simplified

1 pound lamb's quarters
your favorite dressing—butter, vinegar, lemon juice
    or horseradish is suggested
season with dill, rosemary, sage, or marjoram
garnish with bacon bits or grated cheese

Boil the lamb's quarters for 20 minutes. Season and garnish with your favorites. Add your choice of dressing.

Lamb's Quarters, Ramp & Day Lily Soup

2 cups lamb's quarters, chopped
2 cups day lily tubers or potatoes, diced
½ cup ramps (tops & bulbs) or onions, diced
2 tablespoons butter
3 cups milk
3 cups water
2 chicken bouillon cubes
¼ teaspoon sage (optional)

Mix the water and milk together; add the bouillon cubes and cook until the cubes are dissolved. Sauté the ramps in a large saucepan until they are tender. Add the day lily tubers, lamb's quarters, sage, and 3 cups of the chicken broth mixture to the saucepan and simmer for 15 minutes. Add the remaining chicken broth and simmer an additional 5 minutes.

Lamb's Quarters, Day Lily Buds, and Rice

1 cup cooked lamb's quarters (need to use 2
    cups fresh to make 1 cup cooked)
1 cup day lily buds
⅔ cup rice
2 tablespoons butter
soy sauce to taste

Boil the rice in lightly salted water until it is soft. Boil
the lamb's quarters for 20 minutes. Melt the butter
in a saucepan (use a lid), add the day lily buds, and
sauté for 10 minutes over a very low heat. Add the
lamb's quarters and rice to the saucepan and mix
well. Season with soy sauce.

Pokeweed
Phytolacca americana

Poke

Poke or pokeweed *(Phytolacca americana)* may be the most well-known of all the wild food plants. Many folks familiar with this plant simply refer to it as "spring greens" or just "greens." Many valuable plants or beautiful flowering plants are found in North America because the Europeans who first settled our country introduced them for certain beneficial attributes. It is the opposite with poke. Poke is native to much of eastern North America; and once these early Europeans discovered its edibility, they were sending seeds back to Europe where it now is a very common and popular potherb.

This plant can reach a height of eight feet. The stems vary in color from greenish red to deep purple. Its leaves are alternate. The flowers are white and drooping, and the fruit is a deep purple berry.

As a young boy growing up in western Pennsylvania, I used to call poke "ink berry." My friends and I would stain our faces with juice from the berry trying to imitate Indian warriors. Like so many of our wild food plants, the poke must be identified just after it has come up, long before it flowers. There are no comprehensive identification guides available that identify plants in their juvenile stages. Once a patch of poke has been found, make a mental note to visit the same locale at different times during the spring to become familiar with its various growth stages. This is important because of the poisonous aspects of poke. Before elaborating on the edibility and other attributes of poke, a word of warning. Poke can be a dangerous plant if care is not taken when collecting. According to the book, *Human Poisoning from Native and Cultivated Plants* by James W. Hardin and Jay M. Arena, M.D. " . . . This is one of the most dangerous poisonous plants in the United States, because people eat the leaves without proper and complete boiling, or accidently pull up the roots with the leaves." The root is very dangerous. The toxins of the root are said to spread to other parts of the plant as it grows, but the toxins are far less concentrated in the leaves, stems, and fruit.[15]

Don't be afraid to try the poke greens. Any leafy shoots from a plant under eight inches tall are perfectly safe as long as you don't get part of the root with it. Complete boiling is recommended. If you follow these guidelines, you can become "safely" acquainted with a delicious wild food.

Poke tastes much like spinach and is prepared in the same way. It can be eaten with a little vinegar or melted butter, with a cream sauce, or covered with melted cheese.

I have mentioned the poisonous aspects of pokeweed on nature walks by saying, "The only part that is edible are the leaves from plants less than eight inches tall." From time to time I would get a response such as "but I've eaten pickled poke stems," or "the Pennsylvania Dutch make a delicious poke berry pie." This happened often enough for me to realize there must be some substance to these claims. I'm still not sure about the pickled poke stems, but a number of folks I have talked to have eaten poke berry pie. Other texts suggest that the berries either have to be thoroughly cooked or the seeds must somehow be removed to prevent poisoning. I've tasted the berries raw; and they're terrible, but if enough sugar is added, anything will be palatable. I'm not 100% convinced about eating the berries myself, so make sure you are 100% convinced before you try them. I **do not** recommend eating poke berries!

Poke Cream Soup

2 tablespoons butter
2 ramps (tops & bulbs) or small onions, diced
3 tablespoons flour
2 cups water
2 chicken bouillon cubes
1 cup milk
¼ cup non-fat dry milk
1½ cups poke greens, shredded

Mix together the water, milk, and non-fat dry milk; add the bouillon cubes and cook until the cubes are dissolved. Add the poke greens and boil for 5 minutes. While the poke is cooking, melt the butter in a saucepan and sauté the ramps. Add the flour, stirring constantly. Cook for 1 minute; continue stirring. Add the bouillon cube mixture and the poke greens to the saucepan and bring to a boil. Salt and pepper to taste.

Poke Greens

2 quarts poke greens
4 slices bacon, diced
½ cup celery, diced
2 ramps (tops & bulbs), diced
½ cup grated cheese, your favorite

Boil the poke greens until tender (if the taste is too strong, discard the water and boil again), then drain. Fry the bacon until it's crisp; drain off the drippings, and save. Add the poke greens, celery, and ramps to the bacon drippings. Cook over a very low heat (use a lid) for 30 minutes. Sprinkle with bacon and cheese. Serve when the cheese is melted.

Poke Loaf

2 cups poke greens, shredded
2 eggs, slightly beaten
2 tablespoons flour
2 tablespoons butter
1 cup milk
salt & pepper to taste

Boil the poke in 1 quart of water for 5 minutes, then drain. Melt the butter in a saucepan then add the flour. Cook until blended and bubbly. Add the milk and stir until thick and creamy. Pour into a buttered casserole dish; add the poke and eggs. Mix well, salt and pepper to taste and bake at 350° for approximately 40 minutes.

Poke Soup

1½ to 2 cups poke, shredded
3 ramps (tops & bulbs) or 2 medium onions
1 cup Jerusalem artichokes or potatoes, diced
2 tablespoons butter
2 beef bouillon cubes dissolved in 6 cups water
salt and pepper to taste

Wash the poke and cut into strips. Place the potatoes and poke in the beef bouillon broth. Sauté the onions in 2 tablespoons of butter, and add to the soup. Bring the soup to a boil then simmer for 10 minutes. Salt and pepper to taste.

Red Clover
Trifolium pratense

Clover

What do you think of when someone mentions red clover? I think of the buzzing of honeybees and bubblebees, the fragrant smell of the clover nectar and clover honey—so sweet, light and delicate. No wonder the clovers are such a highly esteemed group of plants.

One of the neatest things to do (everybody should have the opportunity to experience these kinds of things) is to go to a great field of red clover in blossom, lie down, close your eyes and relax. There are moments that can change a person's life for all time. This is one of those moments. It's time to go, it's time to eat, it's time to . . . Forget about what it's time to do, just once. I dare you to do it. The buzzing of a bee on a clover flower head right at your ear, the sweet smell of nectar gently carried on a soft, cool breeze. I sometimes feel as if the field is going to swallow me down to the depths of the earth. It may sound frightening, but it's really a peaceful feeling.

The red clover *(Trifolium pratense)* flower is not just a flower, but a compacted head of as many as one hundred or more tiny flowers, each capable of a high nectar yield. No wonder there are so many bees close-at-hand. The fragrance of the flower head has made the red clover popular with weed pickers, nature lovers and wild food enthusiasts. And somewhere along the line somebody decided to do as the bees do, collect the nectar. The best way I have found to do this is as follows:

Clover Tea

1 quart clover flower heads
1 quart boiling water
8 mint leaves
2 teaspoons honey

Suspend the clover flower heads over a pan of boiling water and cover with a lid. As the steam circulates in, on and through the flower heads it pulls the nectar down into the water. After about 5 minutes discard the flower heads and save the water. Sweeten each cup of liquid with ½ teaspoon of honey and add 2 mint leaves. Drink it hot.

Clover tea is especially valuable for coughs and colds. To keep a supply handy, just dry as many clover heads as you think you will need and store in an airtight container.

Clover leaves are a valuable addition to your wild food salad. They are one of the closest things to a complete protein available from plants. That's right, all those clover leaves you walk over or maybe weed from your garden have a great number of the amino acids your body craves. As far as taste goes—there is none. At least my taste buds don't detect any. Several wild food field guides list clover as somewhat indigestible. All the clover leaves that have gone into my mouth have digested, at least I think so. I'm not really sure just how to check to see if they did or didn't.

Some people question the idea of eating something that has no taste. I guess it depends on whether you "live to eat" or "eat to live." If you consider survival the main goal of eating, the addition of clover leaves to your salad will help accomplish that goal. If you are more concerned with putting your taste buds on cloud nine, clover leaves will most likely remain at the bottom of your favorite wild food's list. But remember, although clover leaves won't add to the taste of your salad, they won't take anything away either.

Now for a short detour from the clover's edibility. All clovers are in the pea family and all plants in this family have one special attribute that everybody should know—their roots have tiny, round nodules that are full of nitrogen-fixing bacteria. Nitrogen is one of the most widespread of the elements, but much of it is in the gaseous state. Approximately 70% of the air around us is nitrogen. Now, the trick is to get the nitrogen into the soil in a form that plants can use. This is where the nitrogen-fixing bacteria come in. They take the nitrogen from the air and fix it into the soil. That is why peas or beans should be planted where your corn was growing the year before. Corn needs a lot of nitrogen, and peas and beans replace the nitrogen taken by the corn. Clover works the same way. Many farmers plant clover as a cover crop. In late spring the clover is plowed under and the field is replanted with corn. Pull up a clover plant and check out the roots for yourself. The nodules are easy to see.

The reason the *red* clover has been emphasized in this chapter is due to the larger size of the leaves and flower head. Keep in mind that all those smaller white clovers in the genus *Trifolium* are just as edible.

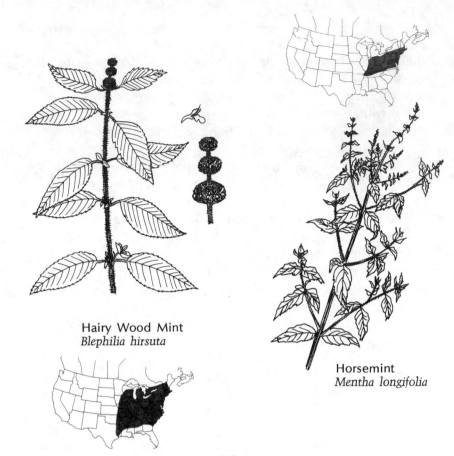

Hairy Wood Mint
Blephilia hirsuta

Horsemint
Mentha longifolia

Mints

All mints have square or squarish stems. I have often heard it said, "if the stem is square, it has to be a mint." Well, just for the record, I have run across several plants with square stems that aren't at all related to the mints—except maybe by the fact that both are in the plant kingdom. But don't get fearful about misidentification and worry about being poisoned. The other plants I know of with square stems are not poisonous; they do not even come close to the aromatic character of the mints for which you will be searching. So what does all this mean? It means that if it is pleasantly aromatic and has a square stem, it is a mint.

Ninety percent of all the "tea mints" I come across are the result of following my nose. Euell Gibbons tells of how he once located a large patch of May-apples by smell alone.[16] It sounds kind of far-fetched, but he wasn't stretching the truth at all. I have a very reliable patch of May-apples that I located by nose alone. Mints can be found in the same way. When I'm in the woods, along a stream, crossing a meadow, wherever, I always break stems and crush parts of plants along the way. It can't be helped. When I tromp through a patch of mints, the aromatic oils quickly reach my nose; and I know what kind of plants I'm passing, just by the smell.

I was once exploring a stream, overturning rocks to see what critters lived there. Occasionally a bird would catch my attention, or I would find a plant I wasn't sure of, and stop to key it out. During one of my "being still" periods (I don't have many) I caught sight of a deer in a meadow about 50 yards upstream. As it walked across the meadow and into the woods, I could smell mints. When I got up, I checked the spot where I was sitting, but no mints. However, when I arrived at the meadow where the deer had crossed, I discovered it was full of mints. The deer had crushed a number of plants, and the wind carried the smell 50 yards to where I had been.

Any mint that is pleasing to your sense of smell generally makes a good tea. I have my favorites, and you'll eventually decide upon yours.

There are only four mints that I collect (unless I'm experimenting): (1) hairy wood mint *(Blephilia hirsuta)*, (2) peppermint *(Mentha piperata)*, (3) spearmint *(Mentha spicata)*, and (4) horse or wild mint *(Mentha longifolia)*. All four of these mints are strongly peppermint-like. I just love to crush the leaves and take a deep breath of the peppermint fragrance. There are other mints in the genus *Mentha*, but the three already mentioned are the only ones common to my area. All make good teas. I collect all my menthas along streams, and we sometimes combine our collecting trips with family outings. My kids are attracted to water like iron to a magnet and while they play along the stream, Bev and I collect mint leaves. The stream becomes the playmate and babysitter all in one. The streams I mention are small and shallow, and Bev and I are close at hand.

The hairy wood mint is more of a woodland species, but occasionally I find it in a damp meadow. It seems to be very common, but my largest patch is only 30 plants. Usually I encounter only 5 to 10 plants at a time.

Collect only the leaves from your mints and only 3 to 4 leaves from each plant. This way you will never deplete an area and have to search out new hunting grounds. One large patch of mints could conceivably supply you for a lifetime if you follow good conservation practices.

And now for some mint history:

According to Pliny, a Roman philosopher: "It will not suffer milk to cruddle in the stomach, and therefore it is put in milk that is drunke, lest those that drink therof should be strangled."[17]

According to Gerard, a very early herbalist: "The smell rejoiceth the heart of man, for which cause they used to strew it in chambers and in places of recreation, pleasure, and repose, where feasts and banquets are made."[18]

Culpepper, a 16th century herbalist, states that: "Being smelled into it is comfortable for the head and memory, and a decoction when used as a gargle, cures the mouth and gums, when sore."[19]

And vegetarians beware: "The smell of Mint does stir up the minde and the taste to a greedy desire of meate."[20]

The Bible tells us (Luke 11:42) that tithes were paid with mints.

Pliny also tells us that the Greeks and Romans crowned themselves with peppermint at their feasts and adorned their tables with its sprays, and that their cooks flavored both their sauces and wines with its essence.[21]

Peppermint is thought to have originated in Hindustan and was taken to Egypt early in written history and spread from there. Again, it may have originated as a variety of the English hairy mint *(Mentha hirsuta)* about 1696. It's superiority over other mints was recognized soon after this date; and by

1750, it was being cultivated on a commercial scale in Europe. It was introduced into this country shortly before the Civil War, at Wayne, New York. By 1855, two acres were under cultivation in Saint Joseph County, Michigan. Just before the depression, this acreage jumped to 35,000, with 1,500 pounds of mint oil to an acre an average yield, valued at $30 a pound. Other states opened up acreage to the plant and its oil came to be second only to turpentine among volatile-oil products in this country.[22]

What I do with my peppermint is:

Mint Tea

1 cup fresh mint leaves
1½ quarts water
one-sixth cup sugar or less

Put the mint leaves into a 1½ quart pitcher. Cover the leaves with 1 pint of boiling water (steep for no more than 5 minutes, then remove the leaves). Add the sugar, 1 quart of cold water chill, then drink to your heart's content.

Spearmint
Mentha spicata

(no illustration)

This last bit of mint information may well be the most significant. Freshly picked mint leaves contain as much vitamin C as its equal weight in oranges and more carotene (pro-vitamin A) than carrots.

You will esteem the mint once you've located a good source and tasted your first cup of mint tea. More mint recipes follow:

Apple-Mint Jelly

4 pounds apples
4 cups strong mint tea
3 cups sugar

Cut the apples into quarters, but do not peel or core. Place them in a large saucepan. Add 1 cup of mint tea per each pound of apples. Bring to a slow boil and simmer for 25 minutes. Place the apples and juice into a jelly bag or several layers of cheesecloth, over a bowl and let it drip overnight. Next morning take 4 cups of the apple mint juice, put in a saucepan and bring to a hard boil. Add 3 cups of sugar and bring to a hard boil again. Stir constantly until jelling point is met (jelling point with a candy thermometer is 220°F or when jelly comes off a spoon in a sheet). Start testing for the jelling point 10 minutes after boiling begins. Pour into ½ pint jars and seal.

Mint Sauce

juice from 1½ lemons
½ cup honey
¼ cup water
pinch salt
10 to 15 fresh mint leaves (chopped)
    or 1 teaspoon of dried (powdered) mint leaves

Mix all the ingredients together and cook for 5 minutes in the top of a double boiler. Add the mint leaves and let everything simmer for 10 minutes. Serve with your favorite meat dish.

Smooth Sumac
Rhus glabra

Fragrant Sumac
Rhus aromatica

Staghorn Sumac
Rhus typhina

Sumac

Of all the beverages made from wild plants, except sassafras, Rhus-aide (also known as "Indian Lemonade") is probably the most popular. I know a number of folks who prefer it over sassafras. The word *Rhus* is the generic name of the sumacs, e.g. staghorn sumac *(Rhus typhina)*, smooth sumac *(Rhus glabra)*, shining sumac *(Rhus copallina)* and others.

Now for those of you who recognize *Rhus* as the generic name for poison ivy, poison oak, and poison sumac—you are absolutely right. But don't be alarmed. Since what you are after is the ripened, red fruit there is no difficulty in identification. Poison ivy, oak, and sumac have greenish fruits that turn white upon ripening. They are never red. Only the edible sumacs have red fruit.

The dominant sumac in my area is the staghorn sumac, and it is easy to locate. It is a sun-loving pioneer plant. Look for it along the edge of fields and roadways. Staghorn sumac is one of the first trees to take up residence on the steep banks of recent road cuts. The word staghorn comes from similarities it shares with a stag's horn (antler) during rutting season. Both are covered with soft, velvet-like hairs.

What you are after from the sumacs is the ripened, red berries. The berries are ripe in the fall and winter. These round, little fruits are clustered by the hundreds at the tip of the branches. The branches are very weak, being composed of a thin ring of wood surrounding a large, soft, pithy center. So if you can't reach the berries from ground level, don't climb, use a ladder. If you try to scale the branches you'll get the berries all right, but you'll also destroy the tree and maybe parts of your own body in the process.

There's one more thing to consider before collecting sumac berries—it's a conservation practice that I call "bluebird conservation." Many folks have the idea that birds like robins and bluebirds and others "all" fly south for the winter. Well most do, but you would be surprised how many stick it out through the cold, snowy winters. I can go out on the coldest day of the year and see as many as 20 robins and often even more bluebirds. This doesn't mean spring is just around the corner. Bluebird flocks will remain all winter in an area where they discover enough ripened sumac berries to support their numbers through the hard winter months. Your overcollecting of sumac berries between November and April can easily interfere with the survival of the flock. The bluebirds and others are having enough difficulties without me or you depleting their winter food supplies. When I'm out tromping the woods during winter and run across some ripened sumac beries, I'm tempted to carry them home for a steaming hot serving of Rhus-aide. But I know that the English sparrows, house wrens, and starlings (all introduced birds) take over bluebird nesting cavities. Also, insecticides have played havoc with the food supply of the bluebirds; and if I collect the sumac berries in the middle of winter, I may add to the problems of the bluebird. For the sake of the bluebird, don't collect sumac berries between November 1 and April 1 unless you live in a warmer climate.

Sumac berries have a taste all their own. They are indescribably refreshing. I love to plop one in my mouth while I'm hiking. It's a great feeling. I know a number of folks who, at first, couldn't get past the tiny hairs that cover the berries. They are so hairy they look like something you'd never put in your mouth. What a lot of people don't know is that these hairs are water soluble. The hairs dissolve when put into water or into your mouth. The hairs are also essential for the good taste provided in a snack of sumac berries.

Rhus-Aide

1 cup ripened sumac berries
1 quart water
one-sixth cup (or less) sugar

Wrap the sumac berries in a piece of cheese cloth and suspend them in a 1 quart pitcher. Add the boiling water and let the berries steep for 5 minutes. Remove the sumac berries, add the sugar, stir and chill. In the middle of winter, serve the Rhus-Aide steaming hot.

Sassafras
Sassafras albidum

Sassafras

Sassafras may be the best known of all wild food plants.

Who has not nibbled the dainty green buds of sassafras in winter, or dug at the roots for a bit of their aromatic bark? Or who has not searched among the leaves for mittens? Surely they are people whose youth was spent in regions that knew not this little tree of the fence corners and woodland borders. And they have missed something very much worthwhile out of their childhood.

from *The Tree Book* by Julia Rogers[23]

I find many young people (about 5th grade age) have heard the name before but are unfamiliar with the use or application of the plant. There are many adults who are able to identify the sassafras tree and who have heard of its reputation as an excellent tea but have never tried it. I've run into professional naturalists who teach about the therapeutic values of sassafras or say things such as "It makes a delicious tea" and yet these teachers have never tried this "excellent brew" themselves. A naturalist who interprets nature but hasn't really experienced it, or a biology professor who teaches from a textbook but has never experienced the "life" they teach about—well, there's something artificial about what these people are doing. Don't just read about sassafras, don't just talk about sassafras; experience sassafras! Take hold of every opportunity to experience the natural world.

I see a God-given relationship between nature and man that I believe can only be truly appreciated through experience. The more a person experiences the natural world, the more this relationship will reveal itself; and as this relationship reveals itself, an "intense" appreciation will begin to develop. I believe there is an infinite wisdom in the natural world that is well beyond man's full comprehension.

We have lost touch with much of the natural world, but we can rekindle that desire to learn more about it through practical outdoor, natural experiences. A cup of sassafras tea is just one of many experiences that has revealed the natural world's significance to me.

I've known a number of older folks who know all about the sassafras, and their knowledge is from first-hand experiences. I can give you a list of reference books about wild foods with a great deal of information, but these older folks can also provide a storehouse of knowledge. Don't make the mistake of being in a hurry to learn about wild foods; be patient and listen to the "experiences" that other people have to share.

Nobody seems to agree as to where the name sassafras originated. The *Flora of West Virginia* states it's an old American

Indian name; *Gray's Manual of Botany* claims the name was first applied by the early French settlers in Florida; and Britton and Brown's *Illustrated Flora of the Northern States and Canada* describes the word sassafras as the popular Spanish name. Although we are not 100% sure who gets credit for the name, we are sure of who's responsible for the great madness that sassafras aroused. In 1577, a book titled *The Joyful Newes from the West Indies* was first translated from Spanish to English. This book was written by Dr. Monardus, a Spanish physician, and listed the medicinal uses of sassafras. The many stories expounded about sassafras were not always true, and many Europeans came to consider this plant as the miracle drug of the time and paid a very high price for a small amount.

Sassafras has lost a lot of its initial prestige since the days of the first explorers into the "new world." But I, and many others, consider sassafras the best of the teas, wild or domestic. Before we go any further, a word of caution from a bulletin put out by the New York State Cooperative Service:

> Many herbal teas are safe substitute beverages for people worried about their caffeine intake, but some have medicinal properties which make them potentially dangerous, especially if drunk in large quantities or strong concentrations.

Sassafras is easy to identify. There are four different leaf shapes, the most common being the shapes of lefthanded and righthanded mittens. If you are still not sure if you have the right plant by the leaf shape, break a twig and take a deep breath. The pleasant odor is distinctive. Look for sassafras in woods, thickets and old fields. I run across individual trees and small groups of larger trees quite often, but what will make your collecting easier and more enjoyable is to find a sassafras grove. A sassafras grove is a large sassafras tree located in an old field where the roots radiate out from the tree for 25 feet or more in all directions. And all along the roots (which can't be seen) there are what appear to be hundreds of smaller sassafras trees. These smaller trees are actually one plant since they all come off of the roots of the larger tree. Science calls them clones; they are all genetically identical. When this condition occurs on fruit trees, we often call them suckers.

When I dig the roots (that's what you are after), I dig from the outside edge of the grove. While I'm digging, my kids are playing hide and seek amongst the smaller sucker trees. Our grove is about 100 feet in diameter; and when someone's hiding in there, you almost need to have a systematic approach to find him. When I have all the root I need (one hour's digging gives me enough root for the whole winter), I go about gathering my kids together. By this time they are hiding from me in the sassafras grove, and if it weren't for their giggles they would be downright hard to find.

Sassafras tea is one of the "easiest" of the wild foods.

Sassafras Tea

10 one-inch pieces of sassafras root, ½ inch in
    diameter
1 quart water
sugar or honey to taste

Once the roots are dug and the dirt rinsed off, put the roots into a 1 quart teapot, bring to a boil, and simmer for 5 minutes. Sweeten with sugar or honey. For a bit stronger tea use only the bark from the roots.

I can get about four or five quarts of tea from one batch of roots. When the flavor begins to weaken, just let the brew steep for about 30 minutes after it's boiled. This can extend the usefulness of the root through a couple more quarts of tea.

Any medicinal benefits that sassafras was once believed to provide are now, for the most part, ignored. There may be some folks tucked away somewhere in the Appalachians who still believe it to be a spring tonic with blood letting capabilities, and it was once believed to prevent and remove the injurious effects of tobacco. Although sassafras has not proven to be a miracle drug, it still brews up a good cup of tea! More sassafras recipes follow.

Sassafras-Mint Jelly

2½ cups strong sassafras tea (double the amount
    used in the tea recipe)
½ cup mint tea
3 ounces powdered pectin
½ teaspoon citric acid
4 cups sugar

Mix the sassafras tea, mint tea, pectin and citric acid. Bring to a boil, stirring constantly, then add sugar. Bring to a boil again. Boil for 1 minute, then pour into ½ pint jars and seal.

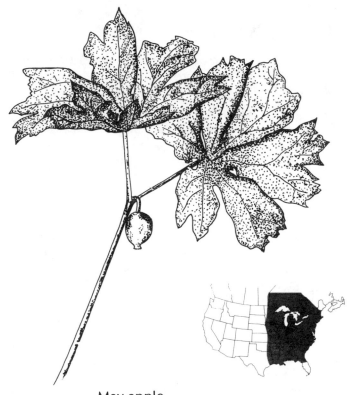

May-apple
Podophyllum peltatum

May-apple

May-apples impress me as being stalwarts of the forest. They occur in troops. Ten here, 75 there, 30 over there, as if they have a duty to protect their own little section of the natural world. And they are very obvious. Basically, the May-apple is a 12-inch flowerless stem terminated by an 8 to 12 inch leaf. The stem is connected to the center of the leaf in umbrella-like fashion. Flowering stems have two lopsided leaves and a nodding, white flower at the center of a forked-stem, making for a very conspicuous creature. The May-apple's presence gives me a sense of security and well-being, as if "all's right with the world."

The May-apple *(Podophyllum peltatum)* isn't an apple at all and, in West Virginia, its ripened fruit is *never* available in May.

It is found most often in rich woods, occasionally in thickets and pastures from Florida to Texas, north to southern Canada. So far we know what it isn't, where to find it, and when not to look for it. A more appropriate name for this plant might be July-berry or August-berry. The ripened fruit is a yellow berry about the size of a golf ball. I collect it from mid-July to mid-August, depending on weather conditions during the growing season.

I have never had difficultly locating the May-apple plant. With no exaggeration, the "troops" are everywhere in the woodlands near my home. The abundance of May-apple plants makes a great first impression, but believe me, the presence of all those plants has little to do with the amount of fruit that will be available. The first time I went collecting May-apples I had great expectations. The size of my bucket showed my optimism. First of all, the majority of the plants I encountered were single stemmed—no flower, no fruit. The plants that had a forked stem and two leaves had a small, dry, shriveled fruit or no fruit at all. I found very few ripened fruits for my bucket. I felt like I do when I go fishing and the weather is perfect, the water's clear, and an occasional lunker-bass swims by but I catch no fish. I got skunked.

I have searched out edible wild plants too late in the season, botched recipes, misidentified plants, and even spent hours foraging only to leave my day's collection lying in the woods somewhere (never to be found) while I go chasing a bird. Learning about the May-apple was a lengthy experience. Since I had come up more or less empty-handed the first year, I was especially careful the second year. While in the woods on other missions I would pay special attention to the May-apples. I located a great many fork-stemmed plants with flowers. I even checked to make sure they were pollinated by examining the ovaries for swelling. I had located hundreds of plants with unripened fruit. Success was imminent. At the proper time I went to collect my treasures. And I found them; my yellow gems were small, dry, and shriveled, just like the year before. I was very discouraged.

After several years of coming up empty-handed, I am now able to go to the woods and, each year, collect all the May-apples I want.

The May-apple is a host of wheat rust *(Puccinia podophylli).* A rust is a fungus that is parasitic upon another plant; and, in the case of the May-apple, it shows up on the leaves as rust spots show up on an aging automobile. The orange-brown rust spots sometimes engulf the whole plant and cause the leaves to curl. But even the slightest sign of rust can cause the fruits to abort before they are fully ripened. That is why several years went by before I had a really successful foraging trip for May-apples. I've since found troops of fork-stemmed May-apples that are rust free and reliable year after year for a large supply of the ripened fruit.

The Modern Herbal Vol. II by Mrs. M. Grieve lists the May-apple under the name American Mandrake and describes the medicinal action of the resin, podophyllin, which can be extracted from the root.

> Podophyllum is a medicine of most extensive service; its greatest power lies in its action upon the liver and bowels. It is a gastro-intestinal irritant, a powerful hepatic and intestinal stimulant. In congested states of the liver, it is employed with the greatest benefit, and for hepatic complaints it is eminently suitable, and the beneficial results can hardly be exaggerated.[24]

Now, before you go out and collect the May-apple root for your own home remedy, get hold of a poisonous plants book and read about the May-apple. With the exception of the ripened fruit, all parts of the May-apple are considered to be poisonous and can cause severe diarrhea and vomiting. Although it is employed as a valuable drug in modern medicine, it should not be used for home remedies.

People are often set in their ways when it comes to trying something different, especially new foods. We have a rule in our home that anything grown in the family vegetable garden has to be eaten by everybody regardless of likes and dislikes. Everybody in our household is very accommodating to this rule. But let someone give us something different to try and it is like pulling teeth getting my kids to take a nibble. They plead, "It didn't come from *our* garden." I call it their food-rule loop-hole. Well, I ran across a tremendous patch of May-apples one year and thought about giving city folks a chance to taste a May-apple. At the time I was working as naturalist in a municipal park with a large out-of-state tourist appeal. I put out a bucket of ripened May-apples with a sign explaining what they were and invited people to try one. I even tried talking people into trying one. After approximately 300 people were exposed to my offer, I gave up, took the May-apples off the counter, threw the sign away, and kept them for myself. Not a single person took me up on my offer. Several people thought they smelled good, but the May-apples never reached a mouth. Because of education or the lack of it, high standards of living, and routine, many folks will never have the opportunity to taste a May-apple or any other wild food.

The people I know who collect May-apples use them in jams and jellies. But if you do want to try your May-apples raw, peel them and discard the skin. The taste is like a cross between a strawberry and a grape, and the pulp and seeds are very grape-like in appearance, only larger.

May-apple Marmalade

1½ pounds May-apples
1 cup water
1 box Sure Jell
5 cups sugar

Cut the stem and blossom ends from the May-apples. Cut the May-apples in half and place them in a large saucepan with 1 cup water. Simmer for about 15 minutes or until the fruit is *very* soft. Strain to remove the seeds and skins. Return 4 cups of the May apple liquid to the saucepan and mix in the Sure Jell. Bring to a hard boil, stirring constantly. Add the sugar and bring to another hard boil, stirring constantly. Boil for 1 minute, skim off the foam and pour into ½ pint canning jars and seal.

May-apple Cookies

½ cup shortening
¼ cup brown sugar
½ cup white sugar
1 cup May-apple pulp
1 egg
2 cups sifted flour
1 teaspoon vanilla
1 teaspoon baking soda
½ teaspoon nutmeg

Cream together shortening, brown and white sugar. Add the May-apple pulp and egg; mix well. Mix together the flour, baking soda, and nutmeg; add to the shortening mixture. Add the vanilla. Roll into small balls, place on a greased cookie sheet, and bake at 350° for 20 minutes. Makes approximately 3 dozen cookies.

May-apple Cake

½ cup shortening
¾ cup sugar
1 cup May-apple pulp
2 eggs, well beaten
¼ teaspoon baking soda
2 cups sifted flour
3 teaspoons baking powder

Cream the shortening and sugar. Add the eggs and May-apple pulp and mix well. Mix together the baking soda, flour, and baking powder; add to the shortening mixture. Stir until smooth. Pour into a greased and floured pan, and bake at 350° for approximately 1 hour.

Multiflora Rose
Rosa multiflora

Pasture Rose
Rosa carolina

Rose Hips

The vitamin C in one cup of rose hips may be equal to the vitamin C in 12 dozen oranges,[25] and one cup of rose hip tea can contain as much vitamin C as six oranges.[26] Of all the nutritious, edible wild plants, rose hips is one of the few that can still be found at the corner drug store: Rose hip vitamin C tablets.

My first introduction with the name rose hip left me somewhat confused. I knew a rose as a beautiful flower, and a hip was the place where my leg connected to my body's main torso. But what was a rose hip? Basically, it is the fruit of a rose bush. I don't know why it is referred to as a hip, but it is. The ripened hips are soft, somewhat wrinkled, and available in the fall of the year and throughout the winter. Anyone who has previously collected rose hips and has memories of an endless chore has probably collected the multiflora rose *(Rosa multiflora)*. The English equivalent of *Rosa multifora* is "many flowered rose," and that is exactly what it is. The small, white flowers are in large clusters and have one of the strongest fragrances of any rose I have smelled—wild or cultivated. There certainly is no shortage of multiflora rose bushes in the wild, but their fruits are very small. The multiflora rose, a native of Japan, is a United States Department of Agriculture approved introduction (though they hate to admit it). It is so thick and thorny that hopes of having it replace barbed wire encouraged its introduction. However, it grows too well, and is an extremely pernicious weed. Everywhere a seed falls (various birds and mammals make sure the seeds fall everywhere) it seems to grow, and the only way to exterminate it is by using dangerous chemicals or by digging it out. Complete removal of the root is essential. Even one root left in the ground can cause the problem to start all over again. To one interested in edible wild plants, the introduction of the multiflora rose doesn't seem too disastrous. It makes more vitamin C available in more places.

The rose hip that I collect is from the pasture rose *(Rosa carolina)*. The pasture rose is found from Florida to Arkansas, north to Nova Scotia, Maine, New Hampshire, Vermont, southern Ontario, Michigan, Wisconsin, Minnesota, and Nebraska. The *Flora of West Virginia* makes mention of the pasture rose being "our most common wild rose." Its fruit, which is much larger than that of the multiflora rose, makes it much easier and less time consuming to pick. Look for the pasture rose in overgrown pastures and along barbed wire fences in open areas. I was collecting hips from a large multiflora rose hedge one winter when I saw a section of the hedge that had enormous hips. I thought I had found a mutation of the multiflora rose and decided to keep a close eye on it during the next spring and summer. To my surprise, instead of finding the small, white, clustered flowers I expected, I found large, pink, solitary flowers. I had encountered my first pasture rose and didn't know it at the time. Once I had positively identified the plant and saw it listed as our most common wild rose, I began to notice it growing in places I pass just about every day. Now I have more available than I need.

Another common, wild rose with large hips is the swamp rose *(Rosa palustris)*. It is found in swamps and lowlands from Florida to Arkansas, north to Nova Scotia and New Brunswick, southern Quebec, Ontario, Michigan, Wisconsin and Minnesota. The wet habitats of the swamp rose sometimes make collecting the hips a cold, wet experience.

If the multiflora, pasture, and swamp rose can't be found in your area, look for the rugosa rose *(Rosa rugosa)*. It was introduced as a garden rose from China a number of years ago and is rapidly taking up residence in many parts of the United States as a wild rose. The rugosa rose has a larger hip than the roses already mentioned, and many foragers may consider it the most flavorful. Check to see if it is common in your area. If you don't have it where you live, it is just a matter of time.

Never trust a rose bush! No matter how careful I am, I seem to get captured by thorns. The thorns on a rose bush are far more dangerous than those on a blackberry or raspberry bush. Even on days I don't remember being caught by the bushes, I somehow end up with punctures and scratches. It's tough to get away without an injury. Be careful!

Rose Hip & Mint Jam

1 cup prepared rose hips*
1½ cups mint tea, unsweetened
juice from 1 lemon
3 cups sugar
1 package powdered pectin

Put the rose hips, ¾ of the cup of tea and the lemon juice into a blender and purée until the mixture is smooth. Slowly add all the sugar to the blender (the blender should be running at a slow speed while the sugar is being added). Purée until all the sugar is dissolved. Add the powdered pectin to the other ¾ cup of tea and boil for 1 minute. Add this liquid to the blender and purée until thoroughly mixed. Pour immediately into ½ pint freezer containers and put into the freezer. Use as needed.

*To prepare rose hips for use in any recipe, cut the stem and flower ends from the hips, cut each in half, and remove the seeds.

A slice of toast with rose hip and mint jam each morning is delicious, but best of all, this breakfast provides the minimum daily requirement of vitamin C.

Rose Hip Syrup

1 cup prepared rose hips
½ cup honey for each cup of rose hip liquid

Put the rose hips in a saucepan* and add enough water to just cover the hips. Put a lid on the saucepan and simmer slowly for 20 minutes. Drain and save the liquid. Repeat the process with the same rose hips. Save this liquid also. Add ½ cup honey for each cup of rose hip liquid. Simmer the mixture until it begins to thicken. Pour the syrup into sterilized jars. Use over pancakes, waffles, etc.

*Use a stainless steel or enamel saucepan. Copper and aluminum can destroy the vitamin C.

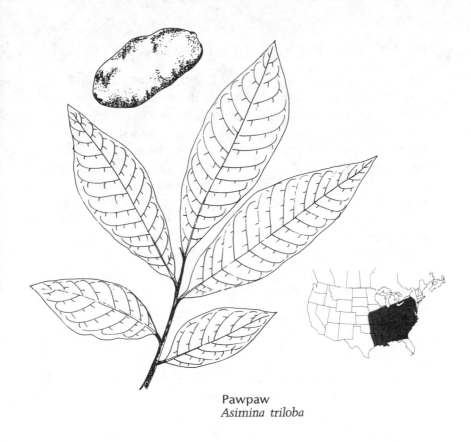

Pawpaw
Asimina triloba

Pawpaws

The botanical name for the pawpaw is *Asimina triloba.* *Asimina* comes from the American Indian name for the pawpaw, assimin; and *triloba* translates as three-lobed in reference to the flower which blooms in April. It resembles the three-cornered hats of colonial times.

The first name I ever heard for this fruit was "West Virginia banana." The pawpaw, a low shrub-like tree, forms a thick undergrowth in many forests, especially throughout the Ohio and Mississippi River valleys. It grows best in rich, moist woodlands and along stream banks. Its northern limits are Ontario and western New York. It extends west to Michigan and southward. The town of Paw Paw in Morgan County, West Virginia was named for this plant.

The only edible part of the plant is the yellow pulp from the fruit. The taste determines the edibility. Some fruits have all the appearances of being ripe: Sweet smell, soft fruit, and a dark brown-black skin. Some fruits which appear ripe leave the mouth with a strange aftertaste when they are eaten raw; however this taste is not present when the pulp from the almost ripe fruit is cooked. The ripe pawpaws are so soft that after peeling, the pulp can easily be removed by squeezing them tightly. The pulp oozes out between the fingers leaving the seeds. This pulp can be mashed or blended to give it a smoother consistency for use in recipes.

The ripened fruit, available from September into October, is three to six inches long, very soft, yellow inside, and has a dark brown to black skin. A ripe pawpaw is unappetizing to the eye but delicious to the taste. I am surprised it isn't a cultivated plant with supermarket appeal. During the fall, it is sometimes sold at roadside stands.

Near my home, solitary trees are rarely encountered. Instead, there are small groves of a dozen or so. Collecting the fruits is somewhat awkward and rarely involves picking the fruits directly off the tree. The trees are too tall to reach the fruit from the ground, it's usually too much work to carry an eight-foot step ladder to where the trees are, and the trees are too skinny and the branches too weak to permit climbing. Since the pawpaw is not a large tree it is relatively easy to dislodge any ripe fruit by shaking the tree rather vigorously. Wear an old hat for protection against gooey, falling objects. The combination of gravity, ripened pawpaws, and a bare head is very messy, especially on a cold day. Fruit gathered off the ground has dirt, small twigs, and leaves embedded in parts of the pulp. Placing pieces of plastic under the crown of each tree before shaking the limbs yields more and cleaner fruit.

When asked to describe the taste of a pawpaw I would say, "It has a taste all its own." This answer proved to be very unsatisfactory so one day I made a thoughtful attempt at a more descriptive answer. It is a combination of a strawberry, pear, and banana with an extra cup of sugar thrown in for good measure. It is so sweet that after two to three bites of the raw fruit I've had plenty; but bake it in a pie or cookie and I can't get enough!

A number of country folks familiar with the pawpaw prefer to eat it baked in the skin like a potato. I prefer it in one of the following recipes:

Pawpaw Bread

3 eggs
1½ cups sugar
1 cup cooking oil
1½ cups pawpaw pulp
3 cups flour
1 teaspoon baking soda
¼ teaspoon baking powder
½ teaspoon cinnamon or nutmeg

Mix all the dry ingredients together. Blend in the eggs, cooking oil, and pawpaw pulp. Mix well. Bake in a greased, floured, bread pan at 350° for 45 minutes to 1 hour.

Pawpaw Oatmeal

½ to 1 cup pawpaw pulp
2 cups oats
4 cups water

Bring 4 cups of water to a boil. Add 2 cups of oats and cook for 5 minutes, stirring occasionally. Add the pawpaw pulp. Stir and serve. Serves six.

Pawpaw Milkshake

¾ cup milk
¼ cup pawpaw pulp
1 to 2 scoops vanilla ice-cream

For each serving combine all the above ingredients and blend until smooth.

Pawpaw Ice-Cream

1 pint vanilla pudding
1 pint pawpaw pulp
1½ quarts milk
1 can sweetened condensed milk
1 teaspoon vanilla

Combine all ingredients in an ice-cream freezer and turn until the ice-cream is stiff.

Pawpaw Cookies

2 cups flour
1 teaspoon baking soda
2 eggs
½ cup shortening
1 cup sugar
1½ cups pawpaw pulp
1 cup chopped hickory nuts or black walnuts
    (optional)

Mix together the flour and the soda. Cream the shortening and sugar then beat in the eggs. To the shortening add the flour and soda mixture and the pawpaw pulp. Add nuts if desired. Bake on a greased cookie sheet at 350° for 15 minutes.

Pawpaw Cake

1 pound butter
2 cups sugar
6 eggs
1 cup milk
2 teaspoons vanilla extract
1 tablespoon baking powder
4 cups white flour
1 cup pawpaw pulp

Blend together butter and sugar with a mixer until light and fluffy. Add 1 egg at a time, blending well after each. Mix the flour and baking powder together. Mix the milk and vanilla together. Add the flour and baking powder mixture (a little at a time) alternating with the milk and vanilla mixture, to the butter, sugar and egg mixture. Mix completely. Add the pawpaw pulp and mix again. Pour into a full-sized, greased and floured cake pan and bake for one hour at 350°

Persimmon
Diospyros virginiana

Persimmons

Persimmons are one of my favorite fruits. They are delicious in bread and cookie recipes. The are also very nutritious and easy to collect. It is said that many early settlers in regions where persimmons were plentiful preferred persimmon bread to gingerbread.

The first order of business is locating a persimmon tree. They are found in dry woods, old fields (my persimmon tree is at the edge of an old field), and clearings from Florida to Texas, northward to New York, Rhode Island, and southern Iowa. The best time to look for *your* tree (wild food foraging can get very personal, especially after going to a favorite spot and finding someone else already there) is after the leaves have fallen from all the trees. The ripened fruit is soft and gooey and remains on the tree well into winter. The usual abundance of one-inch diameter, orange-brown fruit is easy to spot from as far away as 50 yards. In West Virginia, the fruit ripens from late August in the south to mid to late October in the north. The persimmons I collect ripen at about the same time as the first fall frost. This is nothing but a coincidence. Frost is not necessary for ripening as some people believe. Ripeness is determined by taste and anyone biting into an unripe persimmon will never forget the experience. They are so astringent they leave my mouth with the sensation that my tongue is about to swell so large as to clog my throat. Persimmons become less and less astringent as the fruit ripens.

I do all my collecting from an 80 foot tree close to my home. As far as I can determine, I'm the only person gathering the fruit from this particular tree. The sheet of plastic used for catching pawpaws doubles as a persimmon catcher. I spread the plastic under one of the lowest branches and, using a pole pruner, shake the branch vigorously. The fruits are clean, so if your plastic is clean, the only work needed to be done is extracting the pulp. The berries are squeezed through a collander and the seeds and skins that remain are discarded. The pulp can then be frozen, as is, in ½ pint containers. Persimmon size and quality is said to vary from tree to tree, with some trees producing seedless fruit.

Persimmons have a reputation for being an important food for foxes, opossums, and skunks, but I'm not too concerned about competing with wildlife for this wild fruit. I take only three to five percent of the fruit from *my* tree. From my observations, the majority of the remaining fruit ends up on the ground destined to decay.

Persimmon Bread

3 eggs
1½ cups sugar
1 cup cooking oil
1¾ cups persimmon pulp
3 cups flour
1 teaspoon soda
¼ teaspoon baking powder
1½ teaspoons cinnamon
1 cup nuts (optional)

Combine eggs, sugar, cooking oil, and persimmon pulp. Add the soda, baking powder, and cinnamon. Blend well. Add the flour and blend until mixed. Bake at 350° for 45 minutes to 1 hour in a greased and floured bread pan.

Persimmon Cookies

1 cup brown sugar, packed
½ cup shortening
2 eggs
1½ to 1¾ cup persimmon pulp
2¾ cups flour
1 tablespoon baking powder
1 teaspoon cinnamon

Cream the sugar and shortening. Add the eggs and persimmon pulp and mix. Add the baking powder, cinnamon, and flour. Stir until well blended. Drop on an ungreased baking sheet and bake at 400° for 12 to 15 minutes.

Persimmon Chiffon Pudding

2 teaspoons unflavored gelatin
⅓ cup brown sugar (packed)
¼ teaspoon cinnamon
¾ cup persimmon pulp
2 egg yolks, slightly beaten
⅓ cup milk
2 egg whites
¼ teaspoon cream of tartar
¼ cup granulated sugar

Blend the gelatin, brown sugar, cinnamon, persimmon pulp, egg yolks, and milk in a saucepan. Cook over a medium heat until the mixture boils (stir constantly). Water-cool mixture until it will mound when dropped from a spoon. Beat the egg whites and cream of tartar until foamy. Beat in the granulated sugar by tablespoons and beat until stiff and glossy (do not underbeat). Fold in the persimmon mixture and chill several hours before serving.

Persimmon Pancakes

1 cup whole wheat flour
1 cup white flour
2 teaspoons baking powder
1 tablespoon sugar
2 cups milk
2 eggs, well beaten
2 tablespoons cooking oil
½ to 1 cup persimmon pulp

Add all the liquid ingredients to the dry ingredients and stir until well mixed. Add the persimmon pulp. Fry on a hot, greased griddle.

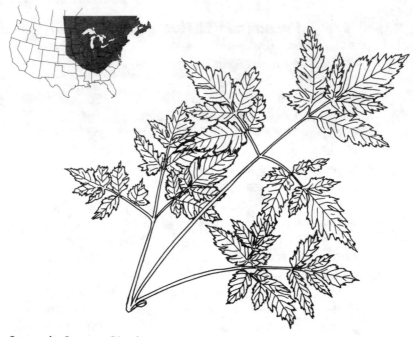

Smooth Sweet Cicely
Osmorhiza longistylis

Sweet Cicely

What would life be without candy? Many dentists would be unemployed, we might be able to work with some of those hyperactive kids, and there would be healthier people in these United States. I'm a rebel when it comes to candy. Halloween candy, Easter candy, Christmas candy, and how often are children rewarded with candy? When you consider what all that sugar can do to a body, it is in reality more of a punishment than a reward. Once a parent gets their kid "hooked" on sugar, it is a war to get them to kick the habit.

Well, there is a two-part solution to this sugar thing. The main part of the solution is being able to say no to "May I have a piece of candy?" That is not always easy when the other kids in the neighborhood are rewarded with sweets, and your kids can't have any. As long as you stay in control of the situation, you'll have victory. Fruit is an excellent substitute for candy, and most kids like fruit. Though it is full of sugar, at least it is not empty calories! When you compare the price of an apple with that of a candy bar, often the former is the cheaper.

The other part of the solution deals with the sweet cicelies. Sweet cicely, aniseroot, sweet anise, and sweet jarvil are all common names used to identify what is known botanically as *Osmorhiza claytoni* (hairy sweet cicely) and *Osmorhiza longistylis* (smooth sweet cicely). *Osmorhiza* is the Greek equivalent for scent root, *claytoni* is for John Clayton, a Virginia botanist, and *longistylis* is Latin for long-styled, referring to a floral characteristic of the plant. Of all the names I have heard for this plant, the one I like best is "candy plant." My oldest daughter was the first person I ever heard use this name.

Green plants make their own food. They take into their systems sunlight, carbon dioxide, and water and transform them into their food, sugar. And in some plants, like the smooth sweet cicely, it is easy to taste that sugar. That is why this plant has all those delicious sounding names.

Sweet cicely grows all through the woodlands near my home, and it is handy enough to gather as a reward in place of candy—and the kids love it. The juicy stem, the leaves, the young seeds, and the root of the smooth sweet cicely tastes just like licorice. The hairy sweet cicely (covered with short hairs) has more of a celery-like taste in all of its aboveground parts. Only the root tastes like licorice. There are two other plants in the genus *Osmorhiza (O. obtusa* and *O. chilensis)* which I have never tried. They are both more northern and western in their range and are said to be similar to their eastern counterparts.

Unfortunately, a word of warning is due with this plant. It is in the carrot family, and there are some poisonous plants represented in this family that are all similar in appearance in their young stages with the candy plant. None of these poisonous plants taste or smell like licorice, and I've never seen them growing with the sweet cicelies. But still—be careful.

My fondest memory of the smooth sweet cicely was during a wild foods workshop I held a while back where one of the participants brought some homemade ice cream flavored with the mild, sweet, anise flavor of the smooth sweet cicely. I couldn't get enough of this ice cream. Even if you don't like licorice candy, give the smooth sweet cicely a try. The anise flavor is very mild. Your kids will love it, and remember those shiny "white" smiles. We all owe it to our kids to do what's best for them.

Smooth Sweet Cicely Ice Cream

Approximately 1 quart of smooth sweet cicely
    stems and leaves
1 quart vanilla pudding
1½ quarts milk
1 can sweetened condensed milk
1 tablespoon vanilla

Mix last four ingredients together in a one gallon ice cream freezer. Put 1 cup of the mixture into a blender and add the cicely (stems and leaves) and purée. Strain and add the liquid to the ice cream freezer. Crank away! Makes 1 gallon.

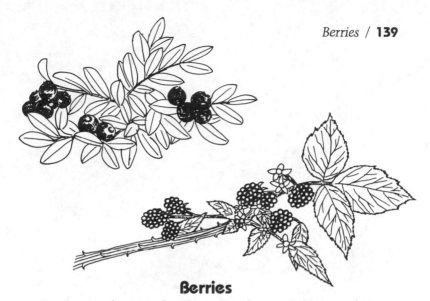

Berries

Berries are fun. My family enjoys berry picking, and I have a better relationship with my wife and children because of our family experiences with berries. I honestly believe that little, seemingly insignificant things like stringing popcorn to put out for the birds in winter, catching crayfish and insect nymphs just for the fun of it, and picking berries for pies and jellies, all add up to (I should say *can* add up to) an opportunity to be together and have fun. If you can allow the kids to get away with such things as eating more berries than they put in the bucket, getting downright wet while exploring a stream, or eating much of the popcorn that the birds were supposed to get, then you are building positive relationships. But if you go out expecting every berry that is found to be put into the bucket for future use, then you would be better off berry picking by yourself. I find this kind of strictness (I'm a great believer in discipline, but not with berry picking.) a strain on the family, and instead of. "I can't wait to go blueberry picking!" it may come out "I don't ever want to do that again." The only reason I mention these things is that I want you (your families, too) to be turned on to wild foods, and I have made many mistakes that you may be able to avoid. I would hate for my kids to grow up disliking the very things I love to do. You wouldn't like it either. Now let's look at some berries.

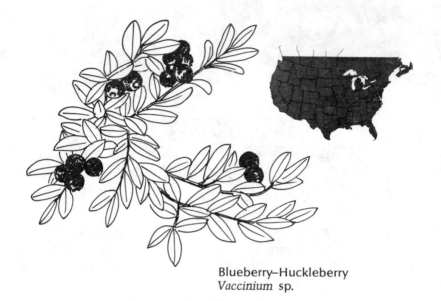

Blueberry–Huckleberry
Vaccinium sp.

Blueberries & Huckleberries

The United States Census Bureau reported that 8,577 quarts of wild blueberries were harvested on private West Virginia land in 1939. Possibly as many more were harvested on National Forest land.[27] Many more are harvested today. I do all my blueberry picking in West Virginia, and I'm sure I'd be included in the statistics of any present day survey the Census Bureau might decide to take.

The blueberry I collect *(Vaccinium vacillans)* is found in dry open woods, thickets, and clearings from Georgia to Missouri, north to western Nova Scotia, southern Maine, southern New Hampshire, Vermont, New York, southern Ontario, Ohio, Michigan, Illinois, and northeast Iowa.

I also pick the black huckleberry *(Gaylussacia baccata)*. Although it is a bit seedy, I prefer it to blueberries. We collect them together since they both ripen at the same time. The black huckleberry ranges from Newfoundland to Saskatchewan south to Nova Scotia, New England, Long Island— New York, Georgia, and Louisiana. *Gray's Manual of Botany* lists 17 species of blueberries and 4 species of huckleberries that occur throughout much of the eastern United States. These berries, of course, as do many of the plants in this book, range throughout the entire United States and Canada. Now, don't worry about being able to distinguish a blueberry from a huckleberry or one species of blueberry from the next. Even professional plant taxonomists and naturalists lose sleep over which is which. They are so similar in taste, size, color, and texture that they are interchangeable in recipes.

We have a box huckleberry *(Gaylussacia brachycera)* in West Virginia that was first discovered by Andre Michaux about 1790 near Berkely Springs, Morgan County. Following this discovery, other locations for the box huckleberry were found near White Sulfur Springs, Greenbrier County about 1800 and Sweet Springs, Monroe County in 1805. These stations, however, were lost to science and the plant was not discovered again until 1921 when F.W. Gray found it in Monroe County. Learning that it was locally known as "juniper berry," he advertised in a county newspaper as to localities in which it could be found and received reports of over 75 localities in 5 counties. It is used for food by people of the region, especially in "juniper berry" pie.[28] The preceeding account should serve as a good example to all wild food enthusiasts having difficulty finding plants that other plant guides list as common. An enormous amount of information can be had from local folks, old-timers, whomever—ask around. Just like West Virginia's mysterious box huckleberry, a lot of valuable information is in the minds of many people and they are often more than willing to share their knowledge.

My family and I take a vacation each year sometime around the third week in July. This corresponds to the blueberry season in the West Virginia highlands. We go backpacking, swimming, sometimes spelunking, but the last day is spent picking in the blueberry and huckleberry fields adjacent to the Dolly Sods wilderness area near Lanesville, West Virginia. Bev and I can pick 20 quarts of blueberries in a day and that's usually more than enough for the next year. We have picked in cold, rainy weather and hot 90° days and always feel well rewarded for the effort. Be prepared—take suitable rain gear and a good hat for protection from the sun.

What do you do with the blueberries you pick? The first thing we do is make a fresh blueberry pie, a sort of a reward for all the berry picking the day before. The remaining 19 quarts are frozen, fresh, just as they are. Don't blanch them. Don't even rinse them off. We pack them in quart bags and pull one from the freezer every time we get a hankering for a pie. Just rinse them off once they thaw and they're ready for whatever. Use them in pies, pancakes, cobblers, muffins, fruit salads, jellies and jams, on ice cream, or just as they are. And most rewarding of all, a hot bowl of granola or cream of wheat on a cold winter morning topped with your very own blueberries.

Blueberry-Maple Soufflé

2 cups blueberries
¼ cup brown sugar
¼ cup maple syrup
3 tablespoons butter
3 tablespoons flour
1 cup milk
4 egg yolks
4 egg whites

Melt the butter in a saucepan. Add the flour and mix completely. Add the milk slowly, stirring constantly, until throughly blended. Bring to a boil while still stirring constantly. Boil for 30 seconds. Remove from the heat, add egg yolks one at a time, and mix with a hand mixer until it's blended. Let the mixture cool. Beat the egg whites until they are stiff. Fold the egg whites into the mixture. Butter a baking dish and sprinkle with sugar. Blend the blueberries, maple syrup, and brown sugar and pour into the baking dish. Cover the blueberries evenly with the soufflé mixture. Bake in a preheated oven at 375° for approximately 40 minutes.

Blueberry Cake

4 cups flour
1 cup blueberries
¾ cup margarine
½ teaspoon baking soda
1½ cups sugar
4 eggs, separated
1 teaspoon cream of tartar
1 cup milk
½ teaspoon grated nutmeg or cinnamon

Mix the butter, sugar, cinnamon or nutmeg, and egg yolks. Mix the flour, cream of tartar, and baking soda. Combine both mixtures slowly and completely. Blend in the milk, add the blueberries and then the egg whites, well beaten. Bake at 350° for 90 minutes or until done in a well greased and floured 9" square cake pan.

Blueberry Muffins

2 cups flour
2 tablespoons baking powder
¼ teaspoon salt
6 tablespoons butter
½ cup sugar
2 eggs
1 cup blueberries

Sift the flour, baking powder, salt and sugar. In a separate bowl beat the eggs and add the butter; mix thoroughly. Add the flour mixture, a little at a time, stirring until it is completely mixed (the batter does not have to be smooth, a lumpy batter is ideal for muffins). Fold in the blueberries. Fill greased muffin tins about two-thirds full. Bake in a preheated oven at 350° for approximately 25 minutes.

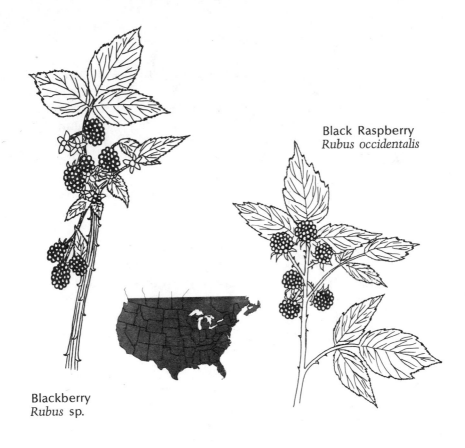

Black Raspberry
Rubus occidentalis

Blackberry
Rubus sp.

Raspberries & Blackberries

Unlike the blueberries which Bev and I travel 150 miles (one way) to pick, the raspberries and blackberries are in walking distance of our home.

If you find it very difficult to distinguish between the 17 blueberry species in the eastern United States, wait till you try the more than 200 blackberries! For the sake of simplicity we will take a close look at the red raspberry *(Rubus strigosis)*, the black raspberry *(Rubus occidentalis)*, and the blackberry in general *(Rubus* sp.) From here on the word blackberry will represent all 200 or so species.

Before we go any futher, a much deserved word about wild red raspberries. There is nothing that compares with them. They are truly indescribably delicious, but they are not nearly as common as the black raspberry and the blackberries. I am forced to collect the red raspberries during the same trip I make for blueberries. They ripen about a week before the blueberries, and I can catch the tail end of the season and "kill two birds with one stone." One 300 mile berry picking trip a year is all I can justify. The red raspberries are found in the more sheltered, damp, somewhat overgrown meadows of the West Virginia highlands, mostly above 3,000 feet. We never bring any home with us. I honestly can't think of any way to improve upon their taste, therefore they are all eaten fresh; no fancy recipes. Look for the red raspberry in thickets, clearings and borders of woods in southern Canada, the northern United States and any eastern state with elevations above 3,000 feet.

I feel safe in assuming that 99.9% of the people who are interested enough in wild foods to read this book are familiar with at least one species in the genus *Rubus*—be it a blackberry or the black raspberry. There are three basic differences that I use to distinguish between the two.

1) The blackberry is larger than the black raspberry. 2) Believe it or not, you can scout out the black raspberries and blackberries long before they flower or fruit. When the fruiting season arrives I don't have to search for the berry patches, I already know where they are. The stem of the black raspberry is round, purplish, and covered with a white powder that readily rubs off. The blackberry stem is four-angled, each angle being round. It looks as if the one stem is really four small, round stems glued together. 3) Here in West Virginia the black raspberries ripen the first of July. The blackberries ripen anywhere from mid-July to mid-August depending on the elevation. We pick every other day over a period of about a week and a half.

Of all the wild food plants that you encounter (except maybe a rose bush), none can be more discomforting than the blackberries. You have to make the decision whether or not the chances you take are worth the pies and jellies you can make. There is poison ivy, thorns galore, sometimes mosquitos, and often hot, muggy weather with which to contend. For protection against poison ivy, I wear G.I. tropical boots, high socks, long pants, and long sleeve shirts. I cover as much of my body as possible. Only my face, ears, neck and hands are exposed. As an added poison ivy precaution, the first thing you should do when you get back home is take your clothes off and take a soapy shower. And don't wear the same berry picking clothes again until they have been washed. I rarely have a problem with mosquitos while berry picking but just the same, my favorite insect repellent is composed of equal parts water and Avon's Skin So Soft mixed together. Besides making me insect free, it makes me smell really good. To avoid the thorns I wear heavy G.I. pants and flannel shirts; but most of all, I'm careful. Those big, ripe berries way down amongst the thorns stay right where they are when I'm picking. The birds can have them. The potato chip commercial says, "I bet you can't eat just one." I can eat just one. I don't have to pick every ripe berry I find. I know some berry pickers who have to get "every one" regardless of the consequences. One lady I know even dons a pair of old hip boots, a rubber raincoat, and a pair of long-wristed gloves to dive right into those briars— she rarely gets a scratch. She does her picking in the evening when it is cooler or on rainy days. To each his own. I also do my picking during the cooler times of the day, 6:00 to 8:30 a.m. and 6:00 to 8:30 p.m. Remember, it is light earlier and longer during the summer, but I can barely take the heat with a flannel shirt on some days even at these hours. I can't imagine wearing a rubber raincoat. If you do pick under the mid-day sun don't forget to wear a wide-brimmed hat.

The same things that you do with blueberries can be done with the *Rubus* species. Pies, jellies, cobblers and much more. But don't forget, individual tastes will determine what you do with your berries. Our raspberries and blackberries go into pies and an all-time favorite with my family for many years, a bowl of milk-covered berries slightly sweetened with sugar. You too, will become well-grounded in your favorite berry recipes.

Black Raspberry Sauce

1 quart black raspberries
1 cup honey
½ teaspoon cinnamon

Squeeze the juice, using cheesecloth, from the raspberries. Blend in the honey and the cinnamon. Use on toast, over biscuits, and on ice cream.

Blackberry Dumplings

1 quart blackberries (the amount depends on how many dumplings are being made and the diameter of the saucepan)
1½ cups flour
2 teaspoons baking powder
3 tablespoons shortening
¾ cup milk

Place the blackberries with sugar (to taste) in a pot and heat to a slow boil. Combine the dry ingredients. Cut in the shortening, then stir in the milk. Drop this mixture, by spoonfuls, onto the hot blackberries and cook uncovered for 10 minutes. Cover and cook until the dumplings are fluffy.

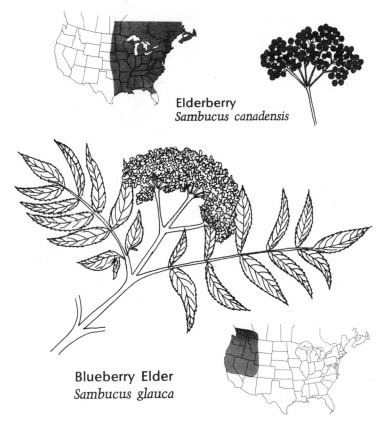

Elderberry
Sambucus canadensis

Blueberry Elder
Sambucus glauca

Elderberries

The common or black elderberry *(Sambucus canadensis)* is found in wet, damp or rich soils from Cape Brenton Island, Nova Scotia to Manitoba, south to New England, Georgia, Louisiana, and Oklahoma. The berries ripen in northern West Virginia about September 7, and they have great holding capacity. There are usually quite a few berries still around to be picked late in September. This chapter is on berries, but there is an excellent wild food available from the elderberry flower. Cut the main stem that holds the whole flower head. Hold the flower head by the stem, dip it into pancake batter, then deep fry. It's excellent and has a delicious, natural sweetness. Kids love elderberry flower fritters. You will too.

As a young boy the elderberry provided me with many mischievous moments. It was one of the first plants I learned to identify. All the boys in the neighborhood would take a foot-long section of the stem, push the soft pith out of the center, and use them as bean shooters. We would all go to the market and buy a package of navy beans then choose sides for a mock war with the bean shooters as the weapons. My favorite bean shooter game took place at the local movie house. We would pay our 25¢ admission and go right to the balcony and search out the prime targets. The prime targets were always bald heads. That game got me into deep trouble more than once!

Bean shooters have become a thing of the past. I can't recall seeing any young people, in recent years, making use of these inaccurate weapons. But it's just as well. In *Human Poisoning from Native and Cultivated Plants* by James W. Hardin and Jay M. Arena, M.D., it states "the roots, stems, and leaves, and much less the flowers and unripe berries, contain a poisonous alkaloid and cyanogenic glycoside causing nausea, vomiting, and diarrhea. Children have been poisoned by making blowguns, whistles, and popguns out of the stems and having them in their mouths. The flowers and ripe fruit are edible without harm and are frequently used for pies, wine, jelly, and pancakes."[29]

I don't know anybody who prefers the black elderberry raw. But if you can find a way to use them raw they are ounce for ounce higher in vitamin C than oranges.[30] To get their truly fine flavor they must be cooked or fermented with a quantity of sugar. It is regrettable that something so pleasing to our taste buds as sugar can be so harmful to our health. The main use we make of the elderberry is in jelly, although many people rave about the pies and wine that can be made.

Now a word about jellies. You can make jelly without sugar. The combination of di-calcium phosphate and low methyl pectin makes this all possible. We have experimented with sugarless jellies with less-than-favorable results. It's hard to break the sugar habit. Unfortunately, in our household, the general consensus is that jelly is not jelly without sugar. Our decision was to eat jelly with the sugar, but we are cutting back on how much jelly we eat. For more information on sugarless jellies write: Walnut Acres, Penns Creek, PA 17826.

Elderberies are deceiving. The very first time Bev and I made elderberry jelly we ended up with 32 ½ pint jars which lasted us five years (we even gave a lot away as gifts). All this from four gallons of elderberies. Only pick what you can use, and knowing how much you can use comes from experience. Bev and I can pick three gallons in one hour. That is if the season is right and the birds haven't discovered them until after we get what we need. There was once a four-year-period when the elderberry crop failed or was eaten very early by birds. But we had our 32 jars of jelly to fall back on!

Elderberries are much smaller than any of the other wild, edible berries. Although they are smaller, they are much easier to gather. One main stem provides a hundred or more berries, and they are easy to separate from the stem . . . that is if you don't mind purple hands (the purple color washes right off). It takes me eight hours to collect 10 quarts of blueberries and about 1 hour for 10 quarts of elderberries.

Elderberry Jelly
3 cups prepared elderberry juice*
4½ cups sugar
1 box fruit pectin
¼ cup lemon juice

Put the prepared elderberry juice, pectin, and lemon juice in a large saucepan or kettle. Measure out the sugar and set it aside. Bring to a full boil, stirring continually. Immediately stir in the sugar. Stir and bring to a full, rolling boil, and boil 1 minute, stirring constantly. Remove from the heat, skim off the foam and pour the jelly into hot glasses or jars. Leave ½ inch head space in glasses or one-eighth inch head space in jars.

Wipe each jar with a damp cloth to remove any excess jelly from the sides, rim, or threads. To seal glasses, spoon one-eighth of an inch of hot paraffin onto the hot jelly surface, making sure that the paraffin touches all sides. Prick any air bubbles in the paraffin seal. Cover with hot lids and screw bands on firmly.

Let the jelly stand to cool. Remove the bands from the jars. Store in a cool, dry place.

Yield: About 4½ cups of jelly from 3 pounds of berries.

*To extract the juice, remove all large stems from the elderberries and crush the berries. Heat gently until the juice begins to flow, then cover and simmer for 15 minutes. Strain the juice through cheesecloth to remove skins, seeds, and small twigs.

Elderberry Flower Fritters

4 elderberry flower heads (6 to 8 inches in
    diameter)
1 cup flour
1 teaspoon baking powder
1 egg
1 cup milk
¼ cup salad oil

Wash the elderberry flower heads and let them dry completely. Heat some salad oil (the oil should be 3 to 4 inches deep) to 375° in a deep fat fryer or electric fry pan. Add the batter ingredients (flour, baking powder, egg, milk, salad oil) into a mixing bowl and beat with an electric mixer. Coat the flower heads with flour. With tongs, dip the flower heads into the batter and let the excess batter drip back into the bowl. Fry each flower head in the hot oil until golden brown.

Large Cranberry
Vaccinium macrocarpon

Cranberries

Four species of cranberries inhabit the eastern United States and Canada, (1) the smaller mountain cranberry *(Vaccinium Vitis-Idaea)*, (2) red-fruited mountain cranberry *(Vaccinium erythrocarpon)*, (3) small cranberry *(Vaccinium Oxycoccos)*, and (4) large American cranberry *(Vaccinium macrocarpon)*.

Cranberries grow in bogs and swamps and they ripen in the fall. Cranberry picking can be very, very wet and cold under those conditions! Not being prepared for adverse weather conditions can ruin what started out to be a fun time. My favorite cranberry patch is about 300 yards from where I pick blueberries. Unfortunately, they ripen at different times of the years. And with gasoline so expensive, we limit our berry picking trip to the mountains to either blueberry season or cranberry season. My family loves blueberries so much that I doubt if we will ever pick cranberries together.

In West Virginia, cranberries are special due to the discovery of a new subspecies *(Vaccinium macrocarpon* Forma *Dahlei)* that doesn't turn red as it ripens—it remains green. I am told that at some future holiday season our cranberry sauce will be available in the Christmas colors, red and green.

Since cranberry bogs are unique due to the rare plants that prefer the acid conditions bogs offer, they are often protected in some way. So before you pick, make sure that what you are doing is not unlawful.

Cranberry Cobbler

1¼ cups sugar
3 tablespoons cornstarch
1 quart cranberries
¼ teaspoon vanilla
1 cup flour
1½ teaspoons baking powder
1 teaspoon sugar
3 tablespoons shortening
½ cup milk

Add 1¼ cups of sugar and the cornstarch in a small saucepan. Mix in the cranberries and vanilla. Cook over a medium heat, stirring constantly, until the mixture thickens and boils. Stir for one additional minute. Pour into a 2 quart baking dish. Mix together, the flour, 1 teaspoon of sugar, and baking powder. Add the shortening and milk and mix well. Drop the dough by spoonfuls onto the hot cranberries. Bake at 400° until golden brown.

Cranberry Pancakes

1 cup whole wheat flour
1 cup white flour
2 teaspoons baking powder
1 tablespoon sugar
2 cups milk
2 eggs, well beaten
2 tablespoons oil
1 cup cranberries

Add all the liquid ingredients to the dry ingredients and stir until well mixed. Add the cranberries. Fry on a hot, greased griddle.

A. canadensis

Serviceberry
Amelanchier sp.

A. alnifolia

Serviceberries

The serviceberry plant (also known as Juneberry) is considered a shrub or small tree, making picking its berries more like picking cherries. The trees are found in thickets and woods from Canada, south to Georgia and Alabama. The ripened fruit is available from June to September depending upon geographical location and elevation.

The name "serviceberry" came about because the circuit-riding preachers would make their rounds, holding church "services," in the mountain communities about the time of the flowering of these beautiful trees. All are in the genus *Amelanchier.*

My first backpacking trip into a designated wilderness area provided a unique and disturbing discovery concerning the serviceberry. Once I made a positive identification and determined its edibility, I began gorging myself with serviceberries. I noticed that just about every tree with abundant fruit had the top five feet or so broken down, making the ripened fruit more accessible. I immediately condemned earlier backpackers for their lack of insight as to what our natural world is all about. These kinds of people shouldn't be allowed out of their houses, let alone granted entry into the wilderness, I ranted. As I went on, I suddenly realized what was responsible for the serviceberry destruction. I was afraid I might catch up with it and that it might be bigger than I. What could I do? I did the same thing most people would do, I got out of that area in a hurry! Broken tops on serviceberry trees are quite characteristic. It is the only way black bears can get the berries.

Serviceberries, although the seeds are much larger, can be used in the same ways as blueberries.

Serviceberry Pie

5 cups serviceberries
⅔ cup sugar
¼ cup flour
½ teaspoon cinnamon
3 tablespoons butter

Line a 10-inch pie pan with your favorite pie crust. Fill with the serviceberries. Mix the sugar, flour, and cinnamon and sprinkle evenly over the serviceberries. Dot with butter. Bake 45 to 50 minutes at 425°.

Wild Strawberry
Fragaria sp.

Strawberries

Picking wild strawberries is becoming a thing of the past. Nurseries and seed companies now offer inexpensive, quality, hybrid plants with big, sweet berries. Many home vegetable gardens now include a strawberry patch, making interest in the wild strawberry almost nil.

The wild Virginia strawbery (*Fragaria virginiana*) is still (in my opinion) tastier than any domestic variety presently available. Unfortunately, it is about one-fifth the size of some of the newer hybrids. The Virginia strawberry is found throughout most of the eastern United States and Canada. For some of you folks who have no room for a strawberry patch, there is a way to get big, "almost wild" strawberries. The common garden strawberry (*Fragaria ananassa*) also occurs as an escape from cultivation in some areas (especially along roads and railroads), and if you can't locate a gone-wild patch, introduce one yourself. But remember, if you put out plants on property other than your own, anyone who finds your strawberries has just as much right to them as you do.

I once planted a strawberry patch in the corner of my vegetable garden and it produced big, juicy berries for me and the robins. I could be picking strawberries in one spot and ten feet away a robin would zip in and steal one of my treasures. When I wasn't in the garden, most of the strawberries would disappear and those that were left were often half-eaten. Frustration occasionally overtook me and a declaration of war against the birds would cross my mind. But I could never carry it out. The birds mean me no harm so why plot evil against them? I finally gave up and plowed under the strawberries and planted vegetables the birds wouldn't bother.

Shortly after I did-in my strawberries, I discovered a natural method for warding off the robins. Although I have no more robin problems, this information will most definitely be retained for my next strawberry patch. Simply put a six-foot pole in the center of the berry patch and a wren house on top of the pole. The problem is solved. House wrens will not stand for any other birds in their territory, they do not eat berries, but they do eat plenty of insects. These birds will guard a strawberry patch and keep harmful insects from the garden all at the same time. Make sure the entrance hole into the wren house is just the right diameter. This will allow the aggressive little house wren to enter and keep the other larger birds from nesting in the house.

Strawberry Pie

2 cups whole strawberries
1 small box strawberry jello
½ cup sugar
1½ cups boiling water
6 tablespoons cornstarch
½ cup water

Mix together the jello and sugar. Add 1½ cups of boiling water. Mix together the cornstarch and ½ cup of water. Add the cornstarch-water mixture to the jello-sugar mixture. Heat, constantly stirring, until clear. Add the strawberries and pour into a pre-baked pie crust. Chill till set.

Strawberry–Banana Milkshake

2 to 3 strawberries
⅓ bananna
¾ cup milk
1 scoop vanilla ice cream

Multiply above ingredients by number of servings. Place in blender and blend until smooth.

Strawberry Jam

5 cups prepared strawberries*
7 cups sugar
1 box powdered fruit pectin

Stir the powdered fruit pectin into the prepared strawberries. Bring to a full boil, stirring constantly. Stir in the sugar, all at once. Stir and bring to a full, rolling boil and boil hard for 1 minute, stirring constantly. Skim off the foam and ladle the jam into hot jars leaving ¼ inch head space. Wipe the threads and sides of the jars with a damp cloth. Cover the jars immediately with hot lids. Screw bands on firmly. Process in a boiling water bath for 5 minutes. Remove jars and let them cool. Check the seals, remove bands, and store in a cool, dry place.

*Wash 2 quarts of strawberries, remove the caps, and crush.

More Recipes . . . !

Wild Fruit Salad

6 pawpaws, pulp only
½ cup English walnuts, minced
½ cup strawberries, sliced
½ cup blueberries

Blend together the pawpaw pulp and walnuts. Separate equally into 3 small bowls. Sprinkle equally, as topping, on all 3 servings, the strawberries and blueberries.

Edible Wild Plant Pie, with Meat or T.V.P.

1 can (10¾ ounces) condensed tomato soup
¼ cup water
2 tablespoons flour
1 teaspoon salt
¼ teaspoon basil
¼ teaspoon peppergrass, chopped
6 small cloves wild garlic, crushed
2 cups hamburger, or T.V.P.*
3 ramps (tops & bulbs), diced
1 pound Jerusalem artichokes, quartered
1 cup day lily buds, chopped
½ cup cheddar cheese, shredded
pie crust for one crust

Blend the soup, water, salt, basil, peppergrass, and wild garlic in a large bowl. Mix in the hamburger (cooked) or T.V.P. Add the ramps, Jerusalem artichokes, and day lily buds. Pour into an ungreased baking dish, 8x8x2 inches. Sprinkle with cheddar cheese. Add a pie crust to the top of the pie. Bake for 20 minutes at 425.° Serves 4 to 6.

*Texturized vegetable protein (T.V.P.) can be found in most health-food stores and co-ops.

Edible Wild Plant Salads

The salads included here are suggestions. They suit my tastes and they are simple. Try these and create your own.

Number 1

½ cup dandelion greens, chopped
½ cup violet leaves, chopped
½ cup purslane
½ cup chickweed leaves
½ cup tuna
5 tablespoons Two-Leaved Toothwort Dressing
    (page 54)

Number 2

1 cup violet leaves, chopped
1 cup chickweed leaves
2 ramps (tops & bulbs), diced
½ cup cottage cheese
salt & pepper to taste

Number 3

1 cup garlic mustard leaves, chopped
¼ cup Cossack asparagus (raw), diced
½ cup chickweed leaves
½ cup of *Cardamine* leaves (any species)
salad dressing, your favorite

Number 4

½ cup watercress leaves
½ cup violet leaves, chopped
2 ramps (tops & bulbs), diced
¼ cup clover leaves
5 tablespoons Peppergrass Oil & Vinegar Dressing
    (page 54)

Number 5

1 cup chickweed leaves
½ cup dandelion crowns
½ cup violet flowers (remove stems)
1 hard boiled egg, diced
salad dressing, your favorite

Number 6

1 cup *Cardamine* leaves (any species)
½ cup violet leaves, chopped
½ cup purslane
2 ramps (tops & bulbs), diced
4 slices bacon, drained & diced
salad dressing, your favorite

A Final Word

Having observed many plants and animals, great and small, I am reminded of a basic philosophy I have come to accept: All living creatures are here for the benefit of mankind, they were specifically put here for our physical well-being, and our existence and their existence was no accident or chance happening.

This philosophy is not what my college professors and textbooks taught me, it is not what I believed in my early post-college career, nor did any person talk me into this way of thinking. But my mind was renewed; renewed by what I have experienced in nature. There is a great and constant communion in process between all of life, and the degree to which we experience this sharing is dependent upon each individual. We have no choice but to accept the communion of plants and/or animals as our only means for food. Green plants are our only oxygen source, and topsoil (dead plants and animals) is the substrate for growing most of our food. Activities such as bird watching, wildlife photography, wild food foraging and others are nothing short of opportunities to enhance this communion.

My hope is that this book will be to you, the reader, an aid to increasing your awareness and participation in this "always available" communion through the study and use of edible wild plants.

But ask the beasts, and they will teach you;
the birds of the air, and they will tell you;
or the plants of the earth, and they will teach you;
and the fish of the sea will declare to you.
Who among all these does not know
  that the hand of the Lord has
    done this?
In his hand is the life of every living thing
and the breath of all mankind.

Job 12:7-10

Literature Cited

1. Margaret Wolfe Hungerford, *Molly Bawn*, Chapter XII.

2. Euell Gibbons, *Stalking the Healthful Herbs*. New York: David McKay Co., 1966. p. 63.

3. Mrs. M. Grieve, *A Modern Herbal, Vol. II*. New York: Dover Publications, Inc., 1971. p. 838.

4. Gibbons, *Stalking the Healthful Herbs*. p. 63.

5. Grieve, *A Modern Herbal, Vol. II*. p. 838.

6. Gibbons, *Stalking the Wild Asparagus*. New York: David McKay, Co., 1962. pg. 57.

7. Ibid., p. 219.

8. Gibbons, *Stalking the Healthful Herbs*. p. 176.

9. Oliver Perry Medsger, *Edible Wild Plants*. New York: Macmillan Publishing Co., Inc. 1966. p. 146.

10. Grieve, *A Modern Herbal, Vol. I*. p. 196.

11. *Favorite Natural Country Foods from the Wilds of the Fifty States, Part II*. West Virginia Department of Agriculture. pp. 10-11.

12. Minnie Watson Kamm, *Old-Time Herbs for Northern Gardens*. New York: Dover Publications, Inc. 1971. p. 31.

13. P.S. Schaffer, William E. Scott, and Thomas D. Fontaine, "Antibiotics That Come From Higher Plants," *Crops in Peace and War*—Yearbook of Agriculture. United States Department of Agriculture, 1950-51. p. 729.

14. Peg Horsburgh, *Science World Magazine*. May 1976, p. 18.

15. James W. Hardin and Jay M. Arena, M.D., *Human Poisoning from Native and Cultivated Plants, 2nd ed.* Durham: Duke University Press, 1974. pp. 70-71.

16. Gibbons, *Stalking the Wild Asparagus*. pp. 128-129.

17. Grieve, *A Modern Herbal, Vol. II*. p. 533.

18. Ibid.

19. Ibid.

20. Ibid.

21. Ibid., p. 537.

22. A. F. Sievers, "Methods of Extracting Volatile Oils from Plant Material and the Production of Such Oils in the U.S." United States Department of Agriculture. *Technical Bulletin No. 16.*

23. Medsger, *Edible Wild Plants.* p. 207.

24. Grieve, *A Modern Herbal,Vol. II.* p. 513.

25. Gibbons, *Stalking the Healthful Herbs.* p. 168.

26. "Mother's Herb Garden—Rose Hips," *The Mother Earth News,* no. 67, January/February 1981, p. 101.

27. P.D. Strausbaugh and Earl L. Core, *Flora of West Virginia.* Grantsville, WV: Seneca Books, Inc. 1977. p. 722.

28. Ibid. p. 720.

29. Hardin and Arena, *Human Poisonings from Native and Cultivated Plants.* pp. 70-71.

30. Gibbons, *Stalking the Wild Asparagus,* p. 87.

Bibliography

Plant Identification Guides

Fernald, Merritt Lyndon. *Gray's Manual of Botany*, 8th ed. New York: Van Nostrand Reinhold Co., 1950.

Gleason, Henry A. *The New Britton and Brown Illustrated Flora.* Lancaster, PA: Lancaster Press, 1952.

Strausbaugh, P.D., and Earl L. Core. *Flora of West Virginia.* Grantsville, WV: Seneca Books, Inc., 1977.

Nutritional Guides

Agricultural Research Service. *Compostion of Foods—Agriculture Handbook No. 8.* United States Department of Agriculture, 1963.

Kirschmann, John D. *Nutrition Almanac.* New York: McGraw-Hill Book Co., 1979.

Shosteck, Robert. "How Good Are Wild Foods?" *The Mother Earth News.* no. 60. Hendersonville, NC. 1979.

Edible Wild Food Guides

Gibbons, Euell, *Stalking the Healthful Herbs.* New York: David McKay Co., 1966.

————. *Stalking the Wild Asparagus.* New York: David McKay Co., 1962.

Grieve, Mrs. M. *A Modern Herbal, Vol. I and II.* New York: Dover Publications, Inc., 1971.

Kamm, Minnie Watson. *Old-Time Herbs for Northern Gardens.* New York: Dover Publications, Inc., 1971.

Medsger, Oliver Perry. *Edible Wild Plants.* New York: Macmillan Publishing Co., 1966.

"Mother's Herb Garden—Rose Hips," *The Mother Earth News.* no. 67. Hendersonville, NC. 1981.

Peterson, Lee. *A Field Guide to Edible Wild Plants.* Boston: Houghton Mifflin Co., 1977.

Poisonous Plant Guides

Hardin, James W., and Jay M. Arena, M.D. *Human Poisoning from Native and Cultivated Plants.* 2nd ed. Durham: Duke University Press, 1974.

Cookbooks

Baker, Ivan. *Delicious Vegetarian Cooking.* New York: Dover Publications, Inc., 1972.

Better Homes and Gardens Books. *Better Homes and Gardens New Cookbook.* Des Moines: Meredith Corporation, 1976.

Crowhurst, Adrienne. *The Flower Cookbook.* New York: Lancer Books, Inc., 1973.

————. *The Weed Cookbook.* New York: Lancer Books, Inc., 1972.

Frederick, J. George. *Pennsylvania Dutch Cookbook.* New York: Dover Publications, Inc., 1971.

Freitus, Joe. *The Natural World Cookbook.* Washington, DC: Stone Wall Press, 1980.

General Mills, Inc. *Betty Crocker's Cookbook.* New York: Western Publishing Co., Inc., 1969.

Longacre, Doris Janzen. *More-with-Less Cookbook.* Scottdale, PA: Herald Press, 1976.

Robinson, Delmar. *Appalachain Hill Country Cookbook.* Charleston, WV: Jalamap Publications, Inc., 1980.

West Virginia Dept. of Agriculture. *Favorite Natural Country Foods from the Wilds of the Fifty States.* Charleston, WV.

Index

Recipe Index